Terry Gifford clarifies the different uses of pastoral, and traces the history of the genre from its classical origins in the poetic dialogues of supposed shepherds, to Elizabethan dramas such as *The Winter's Tale*, through the pastoral poetry of Pope, Wordsworth and Clare, to the more recent rural novels, travel writing and contemporary American nature writing.

Beginning with constructions of Arcadia, the book traces the pastoral impulse of retreat and return using a combination of close reading of quoted texts, cultural studies and eco-criticism. A theory of escape from the circular tension of pastoral and anti-pastoral is offered in the final discussion of texts that are post-pastoral, and Gifford argues that some writers have discovered ways of reconnecting us with our natural environment in an attempt to heal our alienation from nature.

Pastoral is an accessible, succinct and up-to-date introductory text to the history, major writers and critical issues of this genre. Students will find it essential reading.

Terry Gifford is Research Co-ordinator at the School of English, Bretton Hall College of Leeds University. He is author of *Green Voices: Understanding Contemporary Nature Poetry*.

THE NEW CRITICAL IDIOM

SERIES EDITOR: JOHN DRAKAKIS, UNIVERSITY OF STIRLING

The New Critical Idiom is an invaluable series of introductory guides to today's critical terminology. Each book:

- provides a handy, explanatory guide to the use (and abuse) of the term

- offers an original and distinctive overview by a leading literary and cultural critic

- relates the term to the larger field of cultural representation.

With a strong emphasis on clarity, lively debate and the widest possible breadth of examples, *The New Critical Idiom* is an indispensable approach to key topics in literary studies.

- Other books in the series:

PASTORAL

Terry Gifford

LONDON AND NEW YORK

First published 1999
by Routledge
11 New Fetter Lane, London EC4P 4EE

Simultaneously published in the USA and Canada
by Routledge
29 West 35th Street, New York, NY 10001

Routledge is an imprint of the Taylor & Francis Group

© 1999 Terry Gifford

Typeset in Adobe Garamond and Scala Sans by Keystroke,
Jacaranda Lodge, Wolverhampton
Printed and bound in Great Britain by Clays Ltd, St Ives plc

British Library Cataloguing in Publication Data
A catalogue record for this book is available from the British Library.

Library of Congress Cataloguing in Publication Data
A catalogue record for this book has been requested.

ISBN 0–415–14732–8 (hbk)
ISBN 0–415–14733–6 (pbk)

For Gill

Contents

SERIES EDITOR'S PREFACE

The New Critical Idiom is a series of introductory books which seeks to extend the lexicon of literary terms, in order to address the radical changes which have taken place in the study of literature during the last decades of the twentieth century. The aim is to provide clear, well-illustrated accounts of the full range of terminology currently in use, and to evolve histories of its changing usage.

The current state of the discipline of literary studies is one where there is considerable debate concerning basic questions of terminology. This involves, among other things, the boundaries which distinguish the literary from the non-literary; the position of literature within the larger sphere of culture; the relationship between literatures of different cultures; and questions concerning the relation of literary to other cultural forms within the context of interdisciplinary studies.

It is clear that the field of literary criticism and theory is a dynamic and heterogeneous one. The present need is for individual volumes on terms which combine clarity of exposition with an adventurousness of perspective and a breadth of application. Each volume will contain as part of its apparatus some indication of the direction in which the definition of particular terms is likely to move, as well as expanding the disciplinary boundaries within which some of these terms have been traditionally contained. This will involve some re-situation of terms within the larger field of cultural representation, and will introduce examples from the area of film and the modern media in addition to examples from a variety of literary texts.

ACKNOWLEDGEMENTS

My thanks are due to Professor John Drakakis for commissioning a proposal for this book at a dusty conference in Cairo. For his final meticulous editing I am grateful.

Bretton Hall College gave me a semester's reduced teaching in order to work on the book. I am also grateful to the following colleagues who kindly passed on material to me: Ian Dempster, John Brown and Harriet Tarlo.

Professor Fred Rue Jacobs of Bakersfield College, California, also sent me details of new publications with his usual enthusiasm.

I am indebted to Karoline P. Szatek who, as a graduate student at Indiana University of Pennsylvania, gave me her time and later her thesis.

Sabine Ivanovas kindly introduced me to the present pastoralists of Crete in the early morning light of their mountainside.

Jason Aldred, a student at the University of Tennessee, after recovering from the day's Minoan excavations, gave me lucid comments on several chapters as they were written in Mochlos, Crete, where Chris Whitmore of the University of North Carolina, Greensboro, booked my writing room in his 'jewel of a village'.

Louise H. Westling of the University of Oregon offered me books and challenging discussion from which this book benefited greatly.

My partner, Gill Round, deserves special thanks for her patient support and vehement encouragement, first in the French Cervennes, then finally three years later in Crete, and at home in between.

The author and publishers would like to thank the following for permission to use their work: Lawrence Buell for permission to quote from *The Environmental Imagination* (1995); Debjani

Chatterjee for *I Was That Woman* (1989); Jim Crumley for *Among Mountains* (1993); Joe Simpson for *Touching the Void* (1988); Carcanet for Sorley MacLean's *From Wood to Ridge* (1989); Everyman for R. S. Thomas's *Selected Poems* (1997); Faber and Faber Ltd for Ted Hughes's *The Hawk in the Rain* (1957), *Crow* (1970), *Cave Birds* (1975). Excerpts from *Glanmore Sonnets* and *Station Island* from *Opened Ground: Selected Poems 1966–1996* by Seamus Heaney. Copyright © 1998 Seamus Heaney. Reprinted by permission of Farrar, Straus & Giroux, LLC. Excerpts from *Arcadia* by Tom Stoppard. Copyright © 1993 by Tom Stoppard. Reprinted by kind permission of Faber and Faber, Inc. John Murray for George Mackay Brown's *The Wreck of the Archangel* (1989). The lines from *Poem 18* of *Contradictions: Tracking Poems*, the lines from *Poetry III*, from your *Native Land, Your Life: Poems by Adrienne Rich*. Copyright © 1986 by Adrienne Rich. Reprinted by kind permission of the author and W. W. Norton & Company, Inc.

Every effort has been made to contact copyright holders for their permission to reprint material in this book. The publisher would be grateful to hear from any copyright holder who is not here acknowledged and will undertake to rectify any errors or omissions in future editions of this book.

1
THREE KINDS OF PASTORAL

The term 'pastoral' is used in three broadly different ways. First, the pastoral is a historical form with a long tradition which began in poetry, developed into drama and more recently could be recognised in novels. So we can speak of Renaissance pastoral dramas, such as Shakespeare's, or of Augustan pastoral poetry, such as Pope's, and agree that we are talking about a literary form that is used in each of these periods and motifs which we can recognise as deriving from certain early Greek and Roman poems about life in the country, and about the life of the shepherd in particular. Indeed, to refer to 'pastoral' up to about 1610 was to refer to poems or dramas of a specific formal type in which supposed shepherds spoke to each other, usually in pentameter verse, about their work or their loves, with (mostly) idealised descriptions of their countryside. This definition of pastoral is summed up by Leo Marx as 'No shepherd, no pastoral'. For the reader or audience, this literary device involved some form of retreat and return, the fundamental pastoral movement, either within the text, or in the sense that the pastoral retreat 'returned' some insights relevant to the urban audience.

But beyond the artifice of the specific literary form, there is a broader use of 'pastoral' to refer to an area of content. In this sense pastoral refers to any literature that describes the country with an implicit or explicit contrast to the urban. For example, the novels of James Herriot about a North Yorkshire vet could be called pastoral because their country setting is a major presence in the narratives. A poem about trees in the city could also be called pastoral because it focuses upon nature in contrast to the urban context. A delight in the natural is assumed in describing these texts as pastorals. Here a pastoral is usually associated with a celebratory attitude towards what it describes, however superficially bleak it might appear to be.

But that simple celebration of nature comes under scrutiny in the third use of 'pastoral'. A Greenpeace supporter might use the term as a criticism of the tree poem if it ignored the presence of pollution or the threat to urban trees from city developers. Here the difference between the literary representation of nature and the material reality would be judged to be intolerable by the criteria of ecological concern. A farm worker might say that a novel was a pastoral if it celebrated a landscape as though no-one actually sweated to maintain it on a low income. In this case the difference between the textual evidence and the economic reality would be judged to be too great by the criteria of social reality. This is a sceptical use of the term – 'pastoral' as pejorative, implying that the pastoral vision is too simplified and thus an idealisation of the reality of life in the country. Here, what is 'returned' by retreat is judged to be too comfortably complacent to qualify as 'insight' in the view of the user of the term 'pastoral' as a pejorative. So, it remains for the reader to consider whether a James Herriot novel should be characterised as pastoral in having the features of a literary device, or just generally pastoral in content, or pastoral in the critical, dismissive sense.

While this book will clarify each of these uses of pastoral, it will also engage with both the long-standing and the current lively debates around each of these usages. Chapter 2 will trace the origins of the traditional literary form and will define some of the key terms that distinguish different kinds of early pastorals, terms that are often applied to more recent work. Chapters 3 and 4 will discuss the common pattern of the pastoral process of retreat and return, and the last two chapters will show two literary developments, the anti-pastoral and the post-pastoral, that contrast with the traditional pastoral in ways that offer a critique of the convention. Along the way some of the important issues about the pastoral will be discussed, drawing from the recent work of British and American critics. For example, does the pastoral still exist in contemporary writing? John Barrell and John Bull, the editors of *The Penguin Book of English Pastoral Verse*, would say that Herriot's novels cannot be pastorals because, in their view, the historical form of the pastoral is dead and has been since the late nineteenth century when the distinction between the country and the city collapsed: 'The separation of life in the town and in the country that the Pastoral demands is now almost devoid of any meaning. It is difficult to pretend that the English countryside is now anything more than an extension of the town' (Barrell and Bull 1974: 432). Can there really be no twentieth-century continuations of the pastoral form? Must the landscape of the Yorkshire Dales now be described as an extension of the town on the grounds, perhaps, that so many town dwellers now own houses there? Are the shepherds of the Dales engaged in an activity that is in any sense 'an extension of the town'? Is it impossible, then, to even consider any contemporary novels such as Herriot's as pastorals? Could one not argue that the whale and the dolphin have replaced the traditional sheep for a contemporary green poet like Heathcote Williams in *Whale Nation* (1988), his lavishly illustrated long poem, and in *Falling for a Dolphin* (1988), the long poem which followed it? These are questions to which we will return, but the point to note here is that Barrell and Bull are using the term strictly in the primary sense of the traditional literary device.

On the other hand, the editor of the Macmillan Casebook on *The Pastoral Mode* has to admit that, far from being a dead form, there are now so many varieties of pastoral that it has to be regarded as 'a contested term' (Loughrey 1984: 8). Brian Loughrey complains that there is an 'almost bewildering variety of works' to which modern critics attribute the term, ranging from anything rural, to any form of retreat, to any form of simplification or ideal-isation. In this second, more general, sense we can, for example, read in the work of certain critics about 'Freudian pastoral' (Lawrence Lerner), 'the pastoral of childhood' (Peter Marinelli), 'revolutionary pastoralisms . . . like the lesbian-ecofeminist vision of Susan Griffin' (Lawrence Buell), even 'proletarian pastoral' (William Empson) or 'urban pastoral' (Marshall Berman) where no sheep are in sight for miles.

Lawrence Buell, the American critic, has pointed out that 'pastoralism is a species of cultural equipment that western thought has for more than two millennia been unable to do without' (Buell 1995: 32). His term 'pastoralism' is used in the second, more general, sense, of writing 'that celebrates the ethos of nature / rurality over against the ethos of the town or city' rather than 'the specific set of obsolescent conventions' of the original literary form (Buell 1989: 23). If Barrell and Bull are right (and Buell seems to be agreeing with them here) there is, nevertheless, a strong sense that the environmental movement is producing a revival of interest in the writing of new pastoral literature in this general sense. Buell endorses Leo Marx's prediction that the 'wholly new conception of the precariousness of our relations with nature is bound to bring forth new versions of pastoral' (Buell 1995: 51). This will be the focus of Chapter 6, where the best new writing about nature will be seen to actually be an extension of earlier writing that can be defined as having gone beyond the traditional conventions of the pastoral and the anti-pastoral in an alternative 'post-pastoral' vision.

But the development of what Jonathan Bate called 'literary ecocriticism' in his influential book *Romantic Ecology* (1991) has also led to the rereading, through modern ecological perspectives, of earlier literature, such as the pastoral, that engaged with our relationship with the natural environment. Ecocriticism is concerned not only with the attitude to nature expressed by the author of a text, but also with its patterns of interrelatedness, both between the human and the non-human, and between the different parts of the non-human world. A major contribution to this development has been the growth of ecofeminist theory, especially in the USA. Ecofeminist criticism has drawn attention to the gendered nature of the history of our species' 'conquest', control and exploitation of the environment by pointing out that it is the same mind-set that dominated both the environment and women. Indeed, Carolyn Merchant's early work showed that nature and woman have been regarded as interchangeable by scientific thought since the Renaissance. So the more recent development of criticism that has an awareness of our current environmental crisis and its gendered origins will pose new questions for our definitions of pastoral. American ecofeminist poets and novelists, such as Adrienne Rich and Ursula Le Guin, have already been writing new kinds of pastoral that might be defined as such in the primary sense of developing the literary device of retreat and return.

The third, pejorative usage of pastoral has led to contemporary writers, in Britain at least, being reluctant to acknowledge that they are writing in this form at all. There was no such problem in the past since writers expected the reader to accept that certain conventions were at work if the text was declared to be a pastoral from the start. In 1800 Wordsworth published the poem 'Michael', which he subtitled 'A Pastoral Poem' in order to bring a number of assumptions into the mind of the reader. In fact, he then went on to challenge some of the most fundamental pastoral conventions.

However, the poem begins conventionally enough in both content and attitude:

> Upon the forest-side in Grasmere Vale
> There dwelt a Shepherd, Michael was his name;
> An old man, stout of heart, and strong of limb.
> His bodily frame had been from youth to age
> Of an unusual strength; his mind was keen,
> Intense, and frugal, apt for all affairs,
> And in his shepherd's calling he was prompt
> And watchful more than ordinary men.

This shepherd appears to be idealised by the writer in 'unusual strength' and the skill of his craft. But already there is an unexpected attention to his mind, which at two points is implied to be of a broader cast than might be assumed by an urban reader. He is not only 'watchful more than ordinary men' – and perhaps, the separate line implies, in matters beyond his work – but he has developed a mind that is 'apt for all affairs', definitely including those beyond his calling. Wordsworth's shepherd has a maturity, integrity and dignity that is both produced by his work and extends beyond it. The affront to sophisticated readers of poetry in 1800 can be imagined. But Wordsworth goes further in attacking the patronising simplification of a common pastoral convention of the rural worker as bucolic clown. He addresses the reader indirectly:

> And grossly that man errs, who should suppose
> That the green valleys, and the streams and rocks,
> Were things indifferent to the Shepherd's thoughts.
> Fields, where with cheerful spirits he had breathed
> The common air; hills, which with vigorous step
> He had so often climbed; which had impressed
> So many incidents upon his mind

Of hardship, skill or courage, joy or fear;
Which like a book, preserved the memory
Of the dumb animals, whom he had saved,
Had fed or sheltered, linking to such acts
The certainty of honourable gain;
Those fields, those hills – what could they less? had laid
Strong hold on his affections, were to him
A pleasurable feeling of blind love,
The pleasure which there is in life itself.

Characteristically, Wordsworth forces the reader to acknowledge that fear is also present in the joy of this man's life, that experiences of hardship qualify the advantages of the beauty of his environment, but most importantly, that by learning to live with it interactively this lowly worker has achieved the 'honourable gain' of moral responsibility and a fulfilled vitality as a human being that connects him with the life-force itself. So Wordsworth has used the pastoral mode to subvert conventional assumptions about the shepherd by making a realistic and broader portrait of an actual person in an actual village. But is this all that can be said about this poem? What questions might we ask about the writer's role in relation to his subject and his readership?

The pastoral convention has come under attack in recent years as critics have examined the frames within which the writer is presenting a pastoral view of the world. The most serious accusation is the suggestion that pastoral in the seventeenth and eighteenth centuries created a false ideology that served to endorse a comfortable status quo for the landowning class who had been the reading public before the nineteenth century. Perhaps the most comprehensive and succinct attack of this kind is contained in the political definition of pastoral by Roger Sales, which is summed up in his statement that pastoral represents the 'five Rs': 'refuge, reflection, rescue, requiem, and reconstruction' (Sales 1983: 17). His view is that pastoral is essentially escapist in seeking refuge in the country and often also in the past; that it is a selective 'reflection' on past country life in which old settled values are 'rescued' by the text; and that all this functions as a simplified 'reconstruction' of what is, in fact, a more complex reality. The political purpose of pastoral for Sales is slightly more insidious than John Lucas implies when he refers to English pastoral's 'deeply conservative ambition' (Lucas 1990: 118). Sales argues that the literary form came to be used to prevent the questioning of the power structures that underpinned land ownership and, indeed, the complete fabric of society.

When such a view is brought to bear upon 'Michael' one begins to see that the text does still function as an idealisation, and although Wordsworth has introduced new evidence and new criteria for evaluating the life of this shepherd, the writer's role is that of privileged observer who reports from his retreat in the mountains that all is better than well for country workers there. One notices that the text also contains the language of persuasion in details such as those 'dumb animals, whom he had saved' and one wonders if, in such a watchful mind, 'blind love' for fields and hills is quite so sensible. Indeed, the problem of language is one that is central to the accusation of idealisation: how to celebrate without distortion? Wordsworth attempts in the phrase 'blind love' to convey the instinctive harmony that the shepherd has achieved with the non-human world he inhabits. This is the state pursued by contemporary green poets who seek an image that counters human alienation from the earth upon which we depend. The problem is to find a language that can convey an instinctive unity that is at once both prior to language and expressed by a language that is distinctively human. This might be seen as the attempt to reconcile, as all pastoral writers must, David Abram's demand that we reconnect with nature through our sensuous apprehension of it and Gary Snyder's suggestion that language is our natural mode of readjustment. 'Blind love' catches David Abram's part of the human whilst losing the resources of the mind that the writer has been rescuing for the shepherd. 'Michael' can be seen, then, in Sales's terms, as refuge and reconstruction which rescues rural values of an unexpected kind. Wordsworth's great autobiographical poem *The Prelude* reveals that 'Michael' is also a requiem for the poet's childhood, which is reflected upon in *The Prelude* as one in which the young poet himself began to learn those lessons from nature of which 'Michael' is a mature example.

Roger Sales's view of pastoral derives from the pioneering analysis of Raymond Williams in *The Country and the City*. Williams asked questions about the context in which pastoral was written and read. By looking backwards to the only-just-vanished location of many English pastorals, Williams discovered that this was, in fact, a recurring motif and that each only-just-vanished period had *its* pastoral values located in an idyllic recent past when things were less problematic than in the present. As he said of the period of the enclosures, for example, 'an ordered and happier past [is] set against the disturbance and disorder of the present. An idealisation, based on a temporary situation and on a deep desire for stability, served to evade the actual and bitter contradictions of the time' (Williams 1975: 60). For Williams this was an exploitation of the material attractiveness of the rural in order to cover the actual exploitation of the people who lived and worked in the rural landscape. His complaint was that this distortion had become fixed as an 'allegory' so firmly that in 1973 he could write that 'the ordinary modern meaning of pastoral, in the critical discourse of otherwise twentieth-century writers . . . means, we are told, the simple matter in which general truths are embodied or implied' (Williams 1975: 32).

This seems to be a reference to William Empson's famous definition of pastoral as the 'process of putting the complex into the simple' (Empson 1935: 23). For Empson this could include such unrural texts as *Alice in Wonderland* and *The Beggar's Opera* as versions of pastoral because apparently simple and unsophisticated characters of low social status are the vehicle for the writer's exploration of complex ideas about society. Empson arrived at this analysis by observing that 'the essential trick of the old pastoral, which was felt to imply a beautiful relationship between rich and poor, was to make simple people express strong feelings (felt as the most universal subject, something fundamentally true about everybody) in learned and fashionable language' (Empson 1935: 11). But Williams could also be making a reference to the book on pastoral in the first series of 'The Critical Idiom' written by Peter V. Marinelli which develops Empson's notion that a change of location, to the forest of Arden, say, only serves to focus on the problems that have apparently been left behind. For Marinelli 'the pastoral is not by the widest stretch of the imagination an escapist literature in the vulgar sense' (Marinelli 1971: 11) because 'a note of criticism is inherent in all pastoral from the beginning of its existence' (Marinelli 1971: 12). Leo Marx admits that this is not true of *all* pastoral and he seeks to distinguish between two kinds of pastoral, between what he calls 'the complex and sentimental kinds of pastoralism' (Marx 1964: 25), or 'the pastoral of senti-ment and the pastoral of mind' (Marx 1964: 32). Against the popular 'illusion of peace and harmony in the green pasture' that is produced by 'the simple, affirmative attitude we adopt toward pleasing rural scenery' (Marx 1964: 25), Marx posits a vision of a pastoral ideal that requires 'an effort of mind and spirit' (Marx 1964: 70) to achieve. His 'sentimental pastoral' is precisely the escapist, simplistic kind attacked by the pejorative use of the term. His notion of complexity includes the fact that in the best texts of this kind – Shakespeare's *The Tempest* is his example – 'the pastoral design, as always, circumscribes the pastoral ideal' (Marx 1964: 72). There is usually what Marx calls 'a counterforce' undercutting the idyll. The necessity of a return, in other words, in the pastoral design, always leads to a qualification of the idyllic retreat. This is close to Paul Alpers's view that, to the extent that 'shepherds are representative of men' (Alpers 1982: 460), what the pastoral delivers at its best is ultimately an implicit realism.

Marx's book *The Machine in The Garden* is subtitled *Technology and The Pastoral Ideal in America* and it explores what he calls American post-Romantic industrial forms of pastoral. Annabel M. Patterson would regard both Marx and Williams as simply defining the pastoral as historically located ideology. She has shown how each age reinterprets the pastoral in terms of the commentator's ideological values. So the pastoral can be a mode of political critique of present society, or it can be a dramatic form of unresolved dialogue about the tensions in that society, or it can be a retreat from politics into an apparently aesthetic landscape that is devoid of conflict and tension. It is this very versatility of the pastoral to both contain and appear to evade tensions and contradictions – between country and city, art and nature, the human and the non-human, our social and our inner selves, our masculine and our feminine selves – that made the form so durable and so fascinating. Lawrence Buell calls this 'pastoral's multiple frames'. He argues that a careful reading of pastoral in its cultural frame reveals that 'American pastoral cannot be pinned to a single ideological position. Even at its most culpable – the moment of wilful retreat from social and political responsibility – it may be more strategised than mystified' (Buell 1995: 44). His interest is in its 'capacity to assume oppositional forms' within apparently conventional popular 'sleepy safe' visions of America. 'So American pastoral has simultaneously been counterinstitutional and institutionally sponsored' (Buell 1995: 50). There is in American criticism of American pastoral a desire to find in images of the simple life a dual function that is both oppositional and hegemonic. 'American texts', says Buell, 'are particularly susceptible to this because of the ease with which dissent can get co-opted as an aspect of consensus.' The results of this in critical practice can be dramatically aerobic and tend to render any kind of judgement as in danger of missing the point. Although he is rightly dismissive of some of the contemporary environmental apocalyptic books such as the American futuristic writer Ernest Callenbach's famous novel

Ecotopia (1975) as 'forgettable' and 'ephemeral' in quality (Buell 1989: 20), Buell can find this duality in any apparently simplistic passages of Thoreau by a means in which the subtlety of the criticism seems to brilliantly exceed that of the text.

So, with an awareness that there may be different traditions of pastoral, as of pastoral criticism, in the USA, I shall be drawing from both European and US traditions in the texts chosen for discussion here. There are, of course, other post-colonial critiques of pastoral to be made in the literatures that have come under European influence. Buell has discussed some aspects of the pastoral in 'the first African-English novel to be acclaimed a world classic' (Buell 1989: 22), Chinua Achebe's *Things Fall Apart* (1958), for example. The poetry of the contemporary Australian poet John Kinsella, who writes what he has called an 'anti-pastoral' poetry (*Poems 1980–1994*, 1998) deserves examination in relation to fellow Australians Les Murray and Judith Wright whose poetry is rooted in the Australian landscape and draws upon Aboriginal myths embedded in it. But this is an indication of how much more room there is for extending discussion of the pastoral. Pastorals demand alert readings that are capable of making critical judgements about their inner tensions, their contextual functions, their multiple levels of contradictions. They are borderland spaces of activity which can be seen through a number of frames. This is the challenge and excitement that they open up to the reader at a time when a critique of literature that offers constructions of the relationship we might have with and within our natural environment was never more urgent. The traditional pastoral construction of that relationship in pastoral literature is contained in the notion of Arcadia.

2

CONSTRUCTIONS
OF ARCADIA

In the course of writing this book I had an invitation to observe real pastoralism in practice by visiting the shepherds of a village in the mountains of Crete. During the late 1970s an American ethnographer, Michael Herzfeld, had studied the society of this village, which he called 'Glendiot', resulting in his book *The Poetics of Manhood: Contest and Identity in a Cretan Mountain Village* (Herzfeld 1985). He had found that these Cretans believed that they were living a way of life that had a continuity with that of shepherds in ancient Greece. 'They do talk of the birth of Zeus on Mount Ida as though it were historical fact,' wrote the ethnographer (Herzfeld 1985: 35). My single visit focused upon the notion of Arcadia. My conversations with the current ethnographer and with two young shepherds from the village raised some questions about how an idealised, literary notion of place can be used about a real place to express these shepherds' idealisation of their way of life. Was 'Glendiot' Arcadia? When I returned from my visit I wrote what follows in my journal. I offer it as a preface to this chapter.

As dawn broke we were winding up towards the highest mountain villages of western Crete. Driving the four-wheel drive Jeep was the German ethnographer now living in Crete who is studying shepherd culture in these mountains. Sabine Ivanovas sees no reason to doubt that many of the practices she observes today are unchanged in over a thousand years of Mediterranean shepherding. 'Of course,' she says with a smile, 'the shepherds think this *is* Arcadia. And in many ways it actually is.' A maze of dirt tracks beyond the village, getting ever steeper and rougher, brings us to a knoll where a dog is tethered in a wire enclosure. In the cool light of early morning we get out and look around the stony landscape of stunted growth and an occasional thorny tree. Beyond, the highest mountains blanch to sunlit stone. There is no-one in sight, but I have the feeling we are being watched. In these barren hills a week ago a man was shot in a sheep-stealing battle between our men and the next village. Arcadia?

I notice on a distant knoll two men shading their eyes to make us out. Then round the corner come two Greek gods, knee-deep in a black and white sea of goats. That is to say, these two young shepherds walk with the bearing of figures from Minoan frescoes, chest first, jutting chins and brown eyes of liquid fire. But they smile at us shyly. They each have a knife conspicuously bulging from their belts. Sabine knows these brothers and hasn't seen the eldest since he left for the army. 'What did you miss most?' she asks. 'My sheep,' he says. We watch as they feed their goats at rows of low troughs. Only the goats can find anything to eat up here by early August. The sheep have already been herded and taken down to the village for the ninety-five kilometre journey to their winter village by the sea. This used to be a three-day stock drive. Now they spend a month's income on cattle trucks. The boys express contempt for the lowland life. Sabine says that the word they use for it means 'another country; a foreign place'. Being mountain men gives them their aloofness, Sabine says. Arcadia.

They take us higher to their family's hut where they stay for days in summer, milking sheep and making cheese. It is a large stone igloo, watertight and with shelves and benches built into the inner walls. Back in the village, these shy, mild-mannered young men talk with fierce hatred about the next village. 'We may be smaller, but we have all the weapons,' they boast. 'Have you ever seen a Kalashnikov?' One offers to show me his, then thinks better of it. 'They're from China,' they say. 'Every family has one.' Sheep-stealing used to be considered a ritual form of social contact between villages. Perhaps it still is. Perhaps the stories are as exaggerated as the ones their father told to the last ethnographer, Michael Herzfeld. 'There came a point during the fight last week, when we got close to actually firing at each other.' And they still have the witty song competitions too, each singer trying to outdo the other with improvised lines that parody each other or the next village. Arcadia.

* * *

From the beginning of its long history the pastoral was written for an urban audience and therefore exploited a tension between the town by the sea and the mountain country of the shepherd, between the life of the court and the life of the shepherd, between people and nature, between retreat and return. The literary form originates in the *Idylls* of Theocritus (*c.*316–260) whose patron was the Greek general who colonised Egypt in the third century BC. For the sophisticated and decadent court at Alexandria Theocritus wrote a series of poems, based upon the shepherds' song competitions in his native Sicily, that he titled the *Idylls*. For the writer this was a poetry of nostalgia to set against his present life which was actually that of an Alexandrian scholar. What is offered to his patron is a vision of simplicity of life in contact with nature that is vividly evoked with the artifice of poetry:

> The tall air smelt of summer, it smelt of ripeness.
> We lay stretched out in plenty, pears at our feet,
> Apples at our sides and plumtrees reaching down,
> Branches pulled earthward by the weight of fruit.

This is the scene at a harvest festival described by a Sicilian herdsman whose poetic ability is explained by his saying that, having kept flocks in the hills, the nymphs there taught him poetry and song. The hills are still the home of the Muses in the Mediterranean, so this is not unreasonable. But this is not an entirely instinctive gift; his poems do need 'labouring over', as the herdsman puts it. And the strong presence of labour in the *Idylls* is rather ironic since this title has given us the term 'idyllic' which has come to be associated with the pastoral. The word 'idyll' derives from the Greek *eidyllion*, meaning a small picture, and characterises a short poem of idealised description. It is used in a general way, rather than of a specific poetic form. So, for example, not having to harvest fruit or even reach up to pick a plum from the tree would, indeed, be idyllic.

But Theocritus retains a strong and often amusing strain of realism throughout the *Idylls*, as in the case of the making of poetry itself. Herdsmen can only begin an exchange of songs when they have seen to their animals. Life in this country is far from idyllic for the two herdsmen Corydon and Battus, who would not recognise themselves in elegant Renaissance court pastorals which borrow their names. Corydon believes, for all his living at one with nature, that the only language understood by a calf stealing from an olive tree is a heavy stick. He knows that sandals have to be worn in this idyll:

> You shouldn't go barefoot on the hillside, Battus.
> Wherever you tread the ground's one thorny ambush.

These two workers exchange information about grazing techniques in a playful banter that includes a jibe at 'mean-hearted townsfolk' who only deserve the *lean* bull for their sacrifice to Hera. The dual presence in the *Idylls* of town and country, idealisation and realism, celebration and regret, indicates a tension that is fundamental to the 'pastoral space' as Frederick Garber has called it: 'it works with all sorts of gaps that can never be bridged' (Garber 1988: 439). But Theocritus's delight in celebrating the real working context of his herdsmen is actually a glancing back four centuries to the first European literature of country life, Hesiod's *Work and Days*. The complete picture of agriculture and trading presented in *Work and Days* has been narrowed mainly to herding by Theocritus, thereby setting what became a pattern for the later pastoral mode. But importantly Hesiod also looked back to a mythic idyllic time when for mortal men 'the fruitful earth unforced bare them fruit abundantly and without stint'. This is the image of the *Idylls*'s harvest festival and it is, for Theocritus, the transformation of personal nostalgia into a sense of a Golden Age that is given mythic significance.

An additional element of later pastorals that is important to what Theocritus is offering his city readers is the sometimes sad, sometimes comic spectacle of bucolic love. The word 'bucolic', deriving from the Greek *boukolos*, a herdsman, can be used simply to mean 'of the country', but the implications of simplicity of life in this usage have come to be associated with the comic. Sophisticated urban audiences are offered country clowns, for example, in Shakespeare's 'simples' and in Thomas Hardy's 'heath-folk' in *The Return of the Native*. The fifth chapter of Hardy's novel is titled 'Perplexity among Honest People' by which he reveals a patronising tension behind his attempt to dignify the joking, singing, mead-drinking villagers who only have first names.

The reaper named Milton in Theocritus's Idyll 10 complains that his workmate Bacaeus 'can't cut a swathe straight' any more and, when he finds that the cause is love, his cynicism culminates in the advice 'Don't let your feelings get in the way of your work.' The joke here is surely against both reapers. Elsewhere there is a more complex force to the poetry. The result of labouring over composition up in the hills produces lines that are both beautiful and comic in their hyperbole, both alienated and at the same time drawing strength from the environment. In a three-framed effect which keeps the urban reader at a sophisticated distance, Theocritus has his herdsman poet wish to have the poet

> Tityrus by me to sing
> How Daphnis the cowherd sickened for Xenea's love,
> How the hillside shared his pain and how the oaks
> By Himera's banks cried his lament, as he wasted
> Like a snowfall on the slopes of some high mountain
> That lifts its whiteness where we will never climb.

Whilst the high mountain is inaccessible to the cowherd, it is accessible as an image by which to understand the naturalness of his emotional state. The hillside that is his familiar working environment, however, can seem to 'share his pain' in a way that is absurd and yet comprehensible. This degree of intimate environmental interrelatedness, that is clearly understood by the poet, is distanced by the poetic structure and by the hyperbole's hint of humour ('the oaks / By Himera's banks cried his lament'). Theocritus is providing the Alexandrian court with bucolic entertainment. The pastoral is on its way, with its strengths and its weaknesses already in tension, its fundamental contradictions established.

But it was Virgil (70–19 BC) who, two centuries later, writing with the *Idylls* very much in mind, created the literary distancing device of Arcadia that has become the generic name for the location of all pastoral retreats. Arcadia was established in the *Eclogues*, which may be best appreciated in contrast with Virgil's *Georgics*. This latter poem is a practical guide to vegetable and animal husbandry, which description of it might misrepresent the esteem in which it has been held. (Dryden considered it 'the best poem by the best poet'.) In many respects it has much in common with Hesiod's *Work and Days* which Virgil admired. Virgil's detail amounts to a celebration of the farmer's practical skills in working with nature:

> With nature's lead
> Shall man be slow to plant and pay with trouble?
> And, grander trees apart, the humble broom
> And willows there provide both feed for flocks
> And shade for shepherds, fences for sown fields
> And provinder for bees.

The Italian rural community provides for Virgil the source of social values such as piety and hard work. These farmers are prepared to 'pay with trouble' in order to gain from 'nature's lead'. But at the end of this second part of the poem some idealising reflection cannot be resisted. What is significant for the later development of the pastoral is that the idealising of country values is made by Virgil explicitly as a criticism of life in the city:

> But happy too is he who knows the gods
> Of the countryside, knows Pan and old Silvanus
> And the sister nymphs. Neither the people's gift,
> The faces, nor the purple robes of kings,
> Nor treacherous feuds of brother against brother
> Disturb him, not the Danube plotting raids
> Of Dacian tribesmen, nor the affairs of Rome
> And crumbling kingdoms, nor the grievous sight
> Of poor to pity and rich to envy.
> The fruit his boughs, the crops of his fields, produce
> Willingly of their own accord, he gathers.

A shift takes place within this passage from an acknowledgement of the spirits of creativity in the countryside, to a critique of political instability of the city, then to an idealisation of life in the country where the 'pay of labours' has been forgotten. The *Georgics* are not pastoral, taken as a whole. They have given us the generic name for writing that primarily details rural work. But they reveal the process by which a natural enjoyment of working in harmony with the seasons can become, in the pastoral, an idealisation of stability that provides an implicit criticism of turbulent city affairs.

In Virgil's *Eclogues*, his song competitions between shepherds need a distance that will distinguish them from the kind of recognisable realism with which the *Georgics* are to be read. This distance needs to be both literal and literary so that the artifice of his project is transparent to the reader. Bruno Snell has shown that Sicily could not serve this purpose for Virgil because it had become a Roman province 'and her shepherds had entered the service of the big Roman landlords'. These shepherds would be too real and too close to home. So Virgil located the *Eclogues* in what Snell calls 'the humdrum Arcadia' of the Peloponnesus peninsula of Greece. Arcadia is significantly an alpine region that is cut off on all sides by other high mountains. It was the perfect location for a poetic paradise, a literary construct of a past Golden Age in which to retreat by linguistic idealisation. In contrast to the *Georgics*, the Arcadia of *Eclogues* is abstracted from the reality of a working country life. Indeed, in Eclogue IV

> The soil will need no harrowing, the vine no pruning knife
> And the tough ploughman may at last unyoke his oxen.

In fact, Eclogue IV is set in the future when the Golden Age of the past will be restored. This is important because, contrary to some critical opinion, it includes in the scope of the pastoral those utopian Arcadias that project into an idealised future, a restoration of rural values that urbanisation, or industrialisation, or technological alienation from the earth have lost.

The form of the eclogue itself, a brief poem that is either a dramatic monologue or a dialogue, on a pastoral theme, was used four times by Louis MacNeice to comment upon the complacency of the contemporary English society of the early 1930s. In 'Eclogue by a five-barred gate', Death tests the pastoral dreams of two shepherds with a warning: 'your self-congratulation / Blunts all edges, insulates with wool / . . . / This escapism of yours is blasphemy.' Here MacNeice uses the original pastoral form for an anti-pastoral purpose.

But for most classical Latin writers the poetry of an Arcadian Golden Age was located in a primordial past in which human anxieties had not yet surfaced. Having disappeared during the Dark Ages, Arcadia resurfaced in the Italian Renaissance in Jacopo Sannazaro's poem *Arcadia*, first published in Venice in 1502. His utopian Arcadia is described by Erwin Panofsky as 'a realm irretrievably lost, seen through a veil of reminiscent melancholy' (Panofsky 1970: 349). Golding's 1567 translation of Ovid's *Metamorphoses*, shows the importance of this original state, now lost, for the English Renaissance:

> Then sprang up first the Golden Age, which of its selfe maintainde,
> The truth and right of every thing unforst and unconstrained.
> There was no fear of punishment, there was no threatening lawe
> In brazen tables nayled up, to keepe the folke in awe.

Perhaps the significant feature of this text for Elizabethans lies in Ovid's association of his Golden Age with a time before the exploitation of the environment, colonialisation, or urbanisation, all arenas of vigorous Elizabethan activity:

> The loftie Pynetree was not hewen from mountaines where it stood,
> In seeking straunge and ferren landes to rove upon the flood.
> Men knew none other countries yet, than were themselves did keepe:
> There was no towne enclosed yet, with walles and ditches deepe.

Given that most readers of pastoral do themselves live a life of commerce in the town, whether in Elizabethan England, contemporary America, or Horace's classical Italy, Arcadia offers a retreat that even Horace himself, 'the fountainhead of classical pastoral', as Loughrey calls him (Loughrey 1984: 10), finds ironic. In his Epode II Horace's character Alfius dreams of being a farmer instead of a usurer:

> Happy the man, who far from town's affairs,
> The life of old-world mortals shares;
> With his own oxen tills his forebears' fields,
> Nor thinks of usury and its yields.

By the end of Epode II, in which the classical idealised virtues of the country are regaled, Horace mocks his readers' indulgence by revealing that actually Alfius is as cunning in only invoking this vision as a weekender, as he probably is as a moneylender:

> Alfius the usurer, when thus he swore
> Farmer to be for ever more,
> At the mid-month his last transaction ending,
> By next new moon is keen for lending.

The knowing Horace thus wittily reminds his readers that Arcadia is a myth. When we joke about Cretan shepherds today believing that they live in Arcadia, we are referring to the myth of the literary construct. When we say that, actually, it is like Arcadia, we are speaking metaphorically. It is essential to pastoral that the reader is conscious of this construct so that she or he can see what the writer is doing within the device. The ultimate form of this distancing is the pastoral as allegory. The opposite would be to believe that the pastoral vision is reality. The former allows William Empson to say that all allegory is essentially pastoral. The latter allows Roger Sales to accuse eighteenth-century pastoral of social and economic deception. The point is that pastoral is 'carnivalesque' in Bakhtin's sense of playfully subverting what is currently taken for granted: the hegemony of the urban establishment. When pastoral loses that sense of itself as carnivalesque that is so well illustrated by Horace in his coda to Epode II, it becomes dangerously open to exploitation by a culture that might prefer to hide reality in the myth of Arcadia. Was this the function of that strange series of Garden Festivals in Britain during the economic depression of the 1980s? The derelict sites of abandoned industries were turned into gardens that produced no significant source of new employment. Meanwhile a third of the country's employable population were heading for unemployment and another third for work on low incomes. George Puttenham, in one of the first English definitions of pastoral, might have been anticipating in 1589 the government's pastoral project of four hundred years later when he dismissed the pastoral as authentic reality and said that it functions as a 'vaile'.

Puttenham understood that the Golden Age of pastoral was not a historical Arcadia but a literary one:

> Some be of opinion, and the chiefe of those who have written in this Art among the Latines, that the pastorall Poesie which we commonly call by the name by the name of *Eglogue* and *Bucolick*, a tearme brought in by the Sicilian Poets, should be the first of any other, and before the *Satyre*, *Comedie*, or *Tragedie*, because, say they, the shepheards and haywards assemblies & meetings when they kept their cattell and heards in the common fields and forests was the first familiar conversation . . . But for all this, I do deny that the *Eglogue* should be the first and most auncient forme of artificiall Poesie, being perswaded that the Poet devised the *Eglogue* long after the other *drammatick* poems, not of purpose to counterfait or represent the rusticall manner of loves and communication, but under the vaile of homely persons and in rude speeches to insinuate and glaunce

at greater matters, and such as perchance had not bene safe to have beene disclosed in any other sort, which may be perceived by the Eglogues of *Virgill*, in which are treated by figure matters of greater importance than the loves of *Titirus* and *Corydon*. These Eglogues came after to containe and enforme morall discipline, for the amendment of mans behaviour, as be those of *Mantuan* and other moderne Poets.

(Loughrey 1984: 34)

Puttenham also has a sense of the 'carnivalesque' function of the 'vaile' of pastoral. It has an indirectness that enables it to 'insinuate and glaunce' at matters other than those apparently being treated. In other words the Golden Age in the country provides a medium for a critique of the present in the court. He knew that this was what Virgil was about in the *Eclogues* and that the Italian Renaissance poet Mantuan was using the form in this way. This is an ancient function of dramatic narrative art. The anthropologist Paul Radin said of the Native American trickster figure who is the amorally playful character at the centre of a series of folktales, 'He possesses no values . . . yet through his actions all values come into being' (Radin 1956: ix). The trickster figure of Caribbean folktales is Annancy the spider and in the English folk tradition he is the Guiser, the Fool, or the Clown. Shakespeare's shepherds often perform the role of the Clown, and in doing so insinuate a humorous critique of court behaviour, the amendment of which is the subtext of the writer. Thus the pastoral can 'enforme morall discipline', either by recovering values located in the Golden Age, or by a comic critique of the present through the 'vaile' of Arcadia.

One of Puttenham's 'moderne Poets', Sir Philip Sidney, wrote in 1580 in *An Apologie for Poetrie* that the poet 'sometimes, under the prettie tales of Wolves and Sheepe, can include the whole considerations of wrong dooing and patience; sometimes show that contention for trifles can get but a trifling victorie'. His recognition is that the pastoral's critical function is based upon the writer's handling of internal tensions between opposites: 'Wolves and Sheepe', or rather courtiers in wolves' and sheep's clothing. Sydney also shows an awareness that the classical poets were using Arcadia to make social points occasionally, as when the poet 'out of *Melibus* mouth can shewe the miserie of people under hard Lords or ravening Souldiours'. This social criticism is possible, not despite, but because of the artifice of Arcadia: 'Nature never set forth the earth in so rich tapestry as divers Poets have done . . . Her world is brasen, the Poets only deliver a golden.' Of course, Sir Philip Sidney could 'deliver a golden' world himself, as he did in his *Arcadia*, where shepherds display a sophisticated self-consciousness of the Elizabethan use of metaphor:

> Come shepheard's weedes, become your master's minde:
> Yeld outward shew, what inward change he tryes:
> Nor be abasht, since such a guest you finde,
> Whose strongest hope in your weake comfort lyes.

The density of oppositions (shepheard/master; outward/inward; strongest/weake) immediately reveal that this is a Renaissance shepherd who is 'his master's minde'. For him Arcadia is the place in which to explore, supposedly as the classical shepherd Dorus in these extracts, the popular contemporary theme of 'fruitless Love':

> My sheepe are thoughts, which I both guide and serve:
> Their pasture is faire hilles of fruitless Love:
> On barren sweetes they feede, and feeding sterve:
> I waile my lotte, but will not other prove.
> My sheepehooke is wanne hope, which all upholdes:
> My weedes, Desire, cut out in endless foldes.
> > What wooll my sheepe shall beare, whyle thus they live,
> > In you it is, you must the judgement give.

The direct address to the reader invites an objective judgement on the metaphorical 'wooll': the insights gained by this labour on the 'faire hilles' of Sidney's Arcadia. The assumption is that the reader recognises the complicated distancing frame by which this *Arcadia* is constructed. Sydney has first imagined himself as a courtier, a 'master', in earlier times and then dons the 'shepheard's weedes' of classical pastoral. As Barrell and Bull point out, 'his nostalgia is not removed by these two movements back in time – it stays with him, so that he finds himself still looking back to the Golden Age he apparently already inhabits, or to a Golden Age before the Golden Age' (Barrell and Bull 1974: 18). Disappointment remains the only experience of love in *Arcadia*; Sidney himself in the voice of Philisides delivers the judgement: 'You beare no woll, and loss is all my gain'. Nostalgia is all there is in this construct of linguistic and structural abstraction where even the positive images remain unconvincingly asserted:

> Feede on my sheepe, possesse your fruitefull fyeld,
> No woolves dare howle, no murrayne can prevaile,
> And from the stormes our sweeteste sonne will shield.

Raymond Williams steps back further to draw attention to another distancing frame with which this text can be read: 'It is not easy to forget that Sidney's *Arcadia*, which gives a continuing title to English neo-pastoral, was written in a park which had been made by enclosing a whole village and evicting the tenants.' This lends a certain irony to Sydney's nostalgia, in direct contrast to his model, Virgil, who had his farm confiscated and not only includes such experience in his Arcadia in Eclogue IX, but wittily comments upon the inadequacy of pastoral poetry against the forces of social reality: 'Poems such as ours, Lycidas, stand no more chance than doves if an eagle comes.' It is this basis of classical pastoral in the realities of country life, even as it was being reconstructed as literary Arcadia, that was excised from the Renaissance versions of it. That Sir Philip Sidney was not only typical, but himself a model Renaissance pastoral poet, is evidenced by his being the subject of further pastorals by Edmund Spenser.

Spenser's poem *Astrophel* is subtitled *A Pastorall Elegie upon the death of the most Noble and valorous Knight, Sir Philip Sidney*. Sidney had actually died in battle, so it was appropriate to remember him as a knight, but he had appeared in a second, uncompleted, version of *Arcadia* as a Shepherd Knight who had adopted a disguise as a shepherd in order to make an entry at a tournament in an image that was, in Helen Cooper's words, 'a marriage between the lowest and the highest' (Cooper 1977: 145–6). To Spenser this is precisely what Sidney was in the world of feudal heroic romance that Spenser's pastoral inhabits. In the Arcadia of *Astrophel* and *The Faerie Queene* Spenser could take his readers away from the uncertain commercial and political reality of the late Elizabethan court to a more stable only-just-vanished Golden Age. Astrophel/Sidney was 'A Gentle Shepheard borne in *Arcady*', but he acts as a medieval knight performing acts of courage 'in forreine soyle' by which he seeks to win the love of his shepherdess Stella. When he is killed in one of those wicked great foreign forests ('So wide a forest and so waste as this, / Nor famous *Ardeyn*') by 'a cruell beast of most accursed brood', Stella simply leaves her body as a ghost to be his lover in death. Such apparently painless changes are possible in Arcadia, but this is not the end of the story.

> The Gods which all things see, this same beheld,
> And pittying this paire of lovers trew,
> Transformed them there lying on the field,
> Into one flowre that is both red and blew.
> It first growes red, and then to blew doth fade,
> Like *Astrophel*, which thereinto was made.

So by the end of this pastoral Sir Philip Sidney has been transformed from scholar-poet-soldier into shepherd-knight-flower.

Arcadia is a borderland in which not only shape-changing is possible, but also status, role and, in the drama to be discussed in the next chapter, gender changing too. Social uncertainties such as these can be explored within the frame of nostalgic stability such as the feudal rural society of medieval romance. But it was in *The Faerie Queene* that Spenser used this frame to make a social critique of the values of commercial Elizabethan England.

In the sixth book of *The Faerie Queene*, the wandering knight Sir Calidore is taken in by the old shepherd Meliboe, who turns out to be a philosopher with strong views on the Elizabethan preoccupation with making one's fortune by trade and commerce and displaying the results in 'gay showes'. Meliboe says to Sir Calidore,

> 'It is the mynd that maketh good or ill,
> That maketh wretch or happie, rich or poore;
> For some, that hath abundance at his will,
> Hath not enough, but wants in greatest store,
> And other, that hath litle, askes no more,
> But in that litle is both rich and wise;
> For wisdome is most riches: fooles therefore
> They are which fortunes doe by vowes devize,
> Sith each unto himselfe his life may fortunize.'

Sir Calidore is convinced by this rhetoric of Renaissance argument, ending as it does in the brilliant creation of a verb out of a noun to express the creation of a new idea: to 'fortunize' what one has been given, as living riches. (John Gay might have found the invention of 'fortunize' merely a poor attempt to rhyme with 'devize'. In 1714 he wrote about Spenser, 'Yet hath his Shepherds Boy at some times raised his rustick Reeds to Rhimes more rumbling than rural.') Sir Calidore has taken a liking to the old shepherd's daughter, who has the remarkably appropriate name of Pastorella, so he is happy to accept the generosity intrinsic to Renaissance, if not Theocritus's shepherds. But being a courtier, his having been convinced is no guarantee that he has actually understood this shepherd's philosophy.

In fact Spenser has him immediately make two moves which demonstrate that he has fundamentally failed to understand what has been said to him. First he offers the shepherd money and Meliboe has to explain again that 'that mucky masse' is 'the cause of mens decay'. Secondly he sets about courting Pastorella 'With such queint usage, fit for Queenes and Kings, / Ne ever had such knightly service seene'. Pastorella, however, prefers the less ostentatious attentions of the local lad, Coridon. The 'carolings' of the unfortunately named real shepherd Colin Clout are more effective in this Arcadia than Calidore's courtly elaborations of which there is only this to say: 'His layes, his loves, his lookes, she did them all despize'. When Calidore puts on the 'shepheards weed', however, and learns the actual job of herding and even milking the sheep, he wins her love, although this is not finally confirmed until a bit of knightly chivalry in a wrestling contest with his rival Coridon, to whom he is distastefully gracious in victory. A 'natural' social distinction has been confirmed by the text, although the intelligence of the class has been deftly brought into question. Knightly virtues, the intrinsic qualities of good breeding, have ultimately been confirmed, whilst the avarice underlying market values has nevertheless been criticised, if not satirised. It was Ben Jonson who complained in 1636, with ironic wit, of 'an Heresie of late let fall; / That Mirth by no means fits a *Pastorall*'. On the one hand this is a Jacobean jibe at Elizabethan melancholic pastorals such as Sidney's, or the despairing pastorals of Michael Drayton. But to the extent that this is truly a heresy, he might have had in mind Spenser's gentle jokes against Sir Colidore in the sixth book of what has become a classic pastoral of an apparently natural social order.

Ben Jonson was responsible for a shift in a function of pastoral in the seventeenth century that came to a climax in the Augustan pastorals of Alexander Pope. This was the location of Arcadia in the present and in actual country estates. Pastoral could be used to serve a courtly function in praising a patron by describing his effortless management of the country in his ownership. This is, in a sense, the opposite of the georgic because it is significant that nature gives riches to the estate, just as it is natural that the patron has stewardship of the land. The apparently natural social order of feudal Arcadia becomes, in these texts, the natural social order of a supposedly stable present. There are no shepherds in these texts since in these Arcadias nature provides for the deserving, and the poet certainly is no shepherd but a courtier friend in need of a little natural generosity from the aristocracy himself. In 1616 Jonson wrote two such pastorals. The poem 'To Sir Robert Wroth' begins by making the traditional critique of city values:

> How blest art thou, canst love the country, Wroth,
>   Whether by choice, or fate, or both;
> And, though so neere the citie, and the court.
>   Art tane with neithers vice, nor sport.

The poem goes on to list the vices and uncertainties of the court in contrast to the value of security in nature: 'But canst, at home, in thy securer rest, / Live, with un-bought provision blest'.

Pan and Sylvane inhabit this estate, together with less classical forms of entertainment provided for the lord and lady by nature:

> Nor are the *Muses* strangers found:
> The rout of rurall folke come thronging in,
>   (Their rudeness then is thought no sinne)
> Thy noblest spouse affords them welcome grace.

That grace which is so 'natural' to the aristocracy even extends to 'thinking' that the rudeness of rural folk is no sin. In Jonson's time and social position there is no more radical form of generosity possible. The apparent naturalness of all this is summed up by

Jonson in the notion of a lived harmony between people and place, the human in the non-human. For him, to be at one with nature is to be at one with self: 'Thy peace is made; and, when man's state is well, / 'Tis better, if he there can dwell.' Jonson ends his other country-house pastoral of 1616, 'To Penshurst', with a similar notion. The poem concludes with this address to the house itself: 'other edifices . . . / May say, their lords have built, but thy lord dwells'.

'To Penshurst' repeats the emphasis on generosity, passed on from nature's 'free provisions' (both the poet and King James have stayed there, the poem tells us). Again this extends to social toler-ance for 'the farmer and the clowne'. In Thomas Carew's poem 'To Saxham', this reciprocity of natural largesse is celebrated with such deliberate exaggeration that the text is clearly confident that it will not offend, but be regarded as a surface wit that endorses a fundamental truth:

> The Pheasant, Partridge, and the Larke,
> Flew to thy house as to the Arke.
> The willing Oxe, of himselfe came
> Home to the slaughter, with the Lambe,
> And every beast did thither bring
> Himselfe, to be an offering.

And what is being received from nature is returned in spirit to human beings classlessly:

> Thou hast no Porter at the doore
> T'examine, or keep back the poore;
> Nor locks, nor bolts; thy gates have bin
> Made onely to let strangers in.

Raymond Williams has shown how this Arcadia serves to disguise in myth the very opposite that is taking place in reality.

City activity is financing these country houses; the exploitation of nature in these estates is also an exploitation of people; country estates have been produced by the eviction and dispossession of the poor; the myth of rural stability in the seventeenth century is a comfort against the resistance of groups such as the Diggers. Even the titles to estates like these have not been achieved by the innocent gift of nature, but by the very 'vices' this Arcadia of the present opposes. The degree of confidence and bravado that the hyperbole of 'To Saxham' displays might lead one to be suspicious of what it seeks to hide.

Pope made no pretence that his Arcadia of the present in *Windsor Forest* was anything other than a selective reconstruction of reality. In 'An Essay on Pastoral' he wrote (in 1704, he claimed, making him an authority on pastoral at the age of sixteen),

> If we would copy Nature, it may be useful to take this consideration along with us, that pastoral is an image of what they call the Golden age. So that we are not to describe our shepherds as shepherds at this day really are, but as they may be conceiv'd then to have been; when a notion of quality was annex'd to that name, and the best of men follow'd the employment . . . We must therefore use some illusion to render a Pastoral delightful; and this consists in exposing the best side only of a shepherd's life, and in concealing its miseries.

Since Augustan poets like Pope valued the social ideals of order in classical Rome, especially in the reign of Augustus, from whom they derive their name, one would expect to find the Roman gods in their pastorals. But Pope begins *Windsor Forest* with a reference back to the original Arcadia of Christian culture, the biblical Eden. In Eden nature was not wild, but a garden for the delight of Adam and Eve. American Arcadias are usually set, not in a garden, but in a wilderness that is presumed to be in an innocent, original state that is beyond 'the frontier' in both space and time. American

Arcadian innocence is therefore located in a land before colonisation. Indeed, one of the reasons why American critics like Marx (1964) and Buell (1995) are able to take a postive view of the continuing pastoral mode as 'counterinstitutional' (Buell 1995: 50) to a highly materialistic society, is precisely because American nature writing still has expanses of 'wilderness' to sustain its production. Of course, the American vision of its land was created by the colonialists through Eurocentric imagery. Hence the title of Leo Marx's book about the industrialisation of the wilderness in American literature as *The Machine in the Garden*. In the English tradition the image of nature as garden or estate confirms the religiously endorsed right of humans to exploit nature. Eden was the garden that paradise promises to be at the other end of time. In both, humans will be provided for naturally. David Robertson, in his book *West of Eden: A History of the Art and Literature of Yosemite*, in describing the pull of the American West as a kind of Eden, says, 'Our journey to wilderness may, at a deep and even partly unconscious level, be a peculiarly American way of seeking paradise' (Robertson 1984: xvi). Yet the continuing tension between idealisation of Eden as paradise and the desire, or need, to exploit its natural resources in what some American conservationists have called 'wise use', is a tension that still rings through Arcadia.

But Eden also contains the serpent and the apple by which human innocence will be tested. Failing that test leads to another landscape: the city and its vices. The essential quality of Eden is that it is, by definition, a pre-lapsarian Golden Age; after the Fall, the city, the manufacturing from natural resources, the clearcutting of the ancient trees of Eden. (For a post-pastoral response to this process see Rick Bass's 1998 book *Fiber* discussed in the final chapter.) So when Pope suggests that Eden still lives in his description of the present Stuart-owned Windsor Forest, he is not only evoking a religiously endorsed landscape of order, but he is implying that its lord is Lord:

> The Groves of Eden, vanish'd now so long,
> Live in description, and look green in song:
> These, were my breast inspir'd with equal flame,
> Like them in beauty, should be like in fame.
> Here hills and vales, the woodland and the plain,
> Here earth and water seem to strive again,
> Not Chaos-like, together crush'd and bruis'd,
> But, as the world, harmoniously confus'd:
> Where order in variety we see,
> And where, tho' all things differ, all agree.

The Augustan delight in resolving paradoxes, at which Pope is such a master, becomes a vision of the Creation here that is fixed in the landscape itself. The dominant emphasis is on order, but the structure evokes nature's forces in tension. The counterbalances almost become absurd in the zeugma 'harmoniously confus'd', but the following two lines brilliantly explain and justify the conceit. The poetry itself 'strives again', as it were, to recreate Eden out of this landscape's elements. But the function of this construction of original Arcadia is located firmly in 1713 as the poem comes to a clinching climax that might provide a model of the forthrightness of eighteenth-century pastoral's function:

> Here Ceres' gifts in waving prospect stand,
> And nodding tempt the joyful reaper's hand;
> Rich Industry sits smiling on the plains,
> And peace and plenty tell, a STUART reigns.

The final full rhyme, the capitalisation, even the little pause mid-line, all help deliver the poetic punch-line. Now readers can see for themselves why Arcadia can be recognised in the present of 1713.

If *Windsor Forest* relates back to the seventeenth-century Arcadias of Jonson and Carew, Pope's 'Epistles' of the 1730s point forward to the eighteenth-century enthusiasm for landscape gardening and improvement of nature. Pope uses the pastoral conventions in 'An Epistle to Bathhurst' and 'An Epistle to Burlington' to instruct on the moral principles deployed in the construction of an Arcadia for the future:

> Oh teach us *Bathurst*! yet unspoil'd by wealth!
> That secret rare, between th' extremes to move
> Of mad Good-nature, and of mean self-love.

The 'mad Good-nature' of other landowners to which Pope refers is, in fact, an over-generosity in landlords who destroy the woods of their estates in the short-term national interest of providing resources for the navy:

> The Sylvans groan – no matter – for the Fleet:
> Next goes his Wool – to clothe our valiant bands,
> Last, for his Country's love, he sells his Lands.

In his 'Epistle to Burlington' Pope praises Bathurst for investing in a long-term vision of Arcadia:

> Who then shall grace, or who improve the Soil?
> Who plants like Bathurst, or who builds like Boyle.
> 'Tis Use alone that sanctifies Expence,
> And Splendor borrows all her rays from Sense.

This sound Augustan advocacy of reason, discretion and compromise, endorsed still by religion in the word 'sanctifies', is at the service of a vision of Arcadia in the future. Pope's concern is for continued order, represented for him by discretion evident in the planning of the environment's future.

W. H. Auden argued that Arcadia could never be set in the future because there is a fundamental distinction between 'the Arcadian whose favourite daydream is Eden, and the Utopian whose favourite daydream is of New Jerusalem' (Loughrey 1984: 90). Yet other commentators have taken the view that because nostalgia is an essential element of Arcadia, the pastoral is always a backward-looking form. But while this may be true for most pastorals, there is also a more complex set of tensions within the construct. To the extent that pastoral represents an idealisation, it must also imply a better future conceived in the language of the present. Just as the country location enables a direct or indirect critique of the town, and the evocation of a past Golden Age has implications for the present, so this must also have implications for an ideal notion of the future. If this were not the case, the pastoral would lose its oppositional potential. It would not be able to imaginatively construct an alternative vision. Admittedly the force of this oppositional potential will vary, just as the subtlety of its construction will vary, but behind the negative critique within the pastoral there is a positive ideal, and behind the idealisation of the pastoral there is an implicit future. When the pastoral retreats only into a closed past in order to preserve a myth about the present, it has no force for future action. But at its best the pastoral will always imply that its vision of Arcadia has implications for a New Jerusalem.

In fact, when one actually looks at a utopian pastoral such as William Morris's *News from Nowhere*, one finds that much of it is evoking elements of the past in its ideal future. Published in 1890, *News from Nowhere* is set in the year 2102, the year in which its narrator has suddenly woken up one morning, when the industrial cities of Victorian England have been dismantled and people again live in villages or scattered houses surrounded by gardens. It is a socialist utopia, although a peculiarly English one, derived mainly from a marriage of the ideas of Marx and Ruskin. When ownership of land was abolished, 'people flocked into the country villages' and 'yielded to the influence of their surroundings, and became country people; and in their turn, as they became more numerous than the townsmen, influenced them also; so that the difference between town and country grew less and less...' Morris called his novel 'a Utopian Romance' because he had in mind a medieval society of craftsmen and women (the headstone carver in the novel is female). 'All the small country arts of life', which turn work into art and make it such a delight that there is no distinction between work and leisure, have been revived in this neo-medieval village culture. 'The villages of England,' Morris cannot resist pointing out in a deliberate nostalgic reference, 'were more populous than they had been since the fourteenth century.'

So, although it is set in the future, *News from Nowhere*, by reversing the industrial revolution and evoking a neo-medievalism, conforms to any definition of pastoral; this idealised Arcadia is a nostalgic Golden Age which recovers values that are located in the country. (Morris's critique of the city did, in fact, contribute to future change by influencing the town planner Lewis Mumford and the development of the Garden City movement.) In much of its language too, the novel follows the pastoral tradition. Morris invents a kind of dialect for his Arcadian inhabitants that is a simplification of the Victorian love of new words for new ideas or inventions: the revolution in England is called 'the change', or sometimes 'the Great Change', by Morris's Arcadians. A phrase which might be called 'Ruskinian' by Morris's editors, can be seen as relating straight back to the pastorals of Spenser: 'this happy and lovely folk, who had cast away riches and attained to wealth'.

But what is distinctive about Morris from a pastoral perspective is his conception of the human relationship with nature. A young woman in the novel is given a remarkable critique of the nineteenth-century exploitation of nature that links it to a Marxist analysis of the exploitation of people in the 'slavery' of Victorian industrialism:

'Was not their mistake once more bred of the life of slavery that they had been living? – a life which was always looking upon everything, except mankind, animate and inanimate – "nature",

as people used to call it – as one thing, and mankind as
another. It was natural to people thinking in this way, that they
should try to make "nature" their slave, since they thought
"nature" was something outside them.'

The people of 2102, then, are living a life not only in harmony
with nature, but one which fulfils the natural in themselves. Once
again the pastoral, in saying something about the country, is saying
something about society too. Ownership in 2102 does not exist,
especially in human pairings, so there is no marriage in Morris's
utopia. The natural ebbs and flows of emotional attachment
between lovers are acknowledged in Morris's vision of pairings and
partings and re-pairings, as enacted by the two characters Dick and
Clara. This is Morris's view of one of the things that would happen
if humans did not think of nature as 'something outside them'.

As co-inhabitants of the natural world these Arcadians do not
exploit it so much as work with it. The narrative is structured as
a journey up the Thames for the hay harvest. Both the journey
against the current and the harvesting of nature might seem to
suggest the opposite of working with nature. But because there is
no urgency (it is a perpetually sunny summer in Morris's Arcadia)
and because everything is done with the care of a craft-worker,
Morris creates a sense of people not just at ease with their
conditions, but managing them thoughtfully for mutual benefit.
This is sometimes described in terms of aesthetics, which implies
an anthropocentric criteria of management, but for Morris
aesthetics include consideration for the well-being of the material
itself, whether it be stone, or fields, or trees. Here is his narrator's
expression of the management of fields and trees for aesthetics in
this sense, as well as for production:

One change I noticed amidst the quiet beauty of the fields – to
wit, that they were planted with trees here and there, often fruit
trees, and that there was none of the niggardly begrudging of

space to a handsome tree which I remembered too well; and though the willows were often polled (or shrowded, as they call it in that countryside), this was done with some regard to beauty: I mean that there was no polling of rows on rows so as to destroy the pleasantness of half a mile of country, but a thoughtful sequence to the cutting, that prevented a sudden bareness anywhere. To be short, the fields were everywhere treated as a garden made for the pleasure as well as the livelihood of all.

When Engels remarked that Morris was 'a settled sentimental Socialist', he was surely right. But the results of Morris's utopia would have been less disastrous for both the planet and its inhabitants than was Engels's. Morris's decentralised pastoral democracy could not have been so cavalier in its exploitation of the environment as it was clear after 1989 that state socialism had been in Eastern Europe.

Two twentieth-century parallels to Morris's utopian pastoral are to be found in the Northern Californian Arcadias of Ernest Callenbach's 1975 novel, *Ecotopia* and in Ursula Le Guin's 1986 novel *Always Coming Home*. The former is programmatic, journalistic and, in Lawrence Buell's words, of 'forgettable, ephemeral quality' (Buell 1989: 20). Le Guin's more complex book is what she calls an 'archaeology of the future' that includes stories, poems, rituals, music, clothes and customs. Women play a strong part in this society and living in tune with the land and its seasons is a way of marking the seasons of human life as shown in the three-part narrative about a growing girl that forms the backbone of the book. But the overwhelming anthropological material dissipates the force of this utopian narrative.

That contemporary pastoral is not only possible, but is an essential element in the culture of each of the countries that comprise the archipelago of Britain and Ireland, can be demonstrated in aspects of the poetry of Norman Nicholson from

England, John Montague from Ireland, R. S. Thomas from Wales and George Mackay Brown from Scotland. Nicholson's poetry finds a cosiness in the constancy of his Cumbrian mountains and in the nostalgia for childhood that reaches for the same effects as Georgian pastoral verse. Despite apparent movement and change in the landscapes of his poetry, the final emphasis is on a reliable kind of stasis, like 'Scafell Pike / Still there'. John Montague is not beyond explicitly wishing for a return to Goldsmith's Arcadia in the face of the Troubles in the North of Ireland in the 'Epilogue' to *The Rough Field* (1989). It is a classic feature of pastoral that the golden age of Arcadia is only just 'going / going / GONE' in the words of fatalistic loss with which Montague concludes his ambitious long poem. R. S. Thomas's 'pessimistic pastoral', as Barrell and Bull called it, was embedded in the bleak melancholy of his early poetry, but has given way to a later search for God in the Welsh fields. The improvement in the weather between the grim 'Welsh Landscape' and 'The Bright Field', between 'A Peasant' and 'The Moor', indicates that Thomas has finally allowed himself the idyll in nature that he had been both resisting and desiring in his lifetime's religious quest.

But the most consistent and classical Arcadia constructed in the work of these poets is that of George Mackay Brown's use of his native Orkney, which resembles, in many respects, Oliver Goldsmith's construct of 'Auburn' in his eighteenth-century pastoral *The Deserted Village*. Mackay Brown's entire *œuvre* of stories and poems are set in Orkney, where he lived all his life, except for a period at university in Edinburgh. In 1989, at the age of sixty-seven, he made his first visit to England. But his poetry is actually set in an Orkney of the past. 'Modern Orkney,' he has said, 'has little of the stuff of poetry . . . Too many machines, pre-packaging etcetera. Also newspapers . . . T.V.' In a remarkably revealing statement he located his pastoral Orkney as a nostalgic construct: 'When I write of the present it is always thirty or forty years ago or set in my childhood.' In the Introduction to his collection *Fishermen with Ploughs* the poet blames the 'new altars' of 'Progress' for the depopulation of the Rackwick valley on the island of Hoy where this cycle of poems is set. He twice uses the word 'myth' to refer to his narrative in these poems. The poems evoke a time before 'Progress' when people lived in harmony with the seasons and the elements of this place. Winters were tough, but because the cycle of harmony dominates, this is acceptable in its inevitability. The problem is that experience becomes un-differentiated, as 'ice' is simply counterbalanced by 'fire' in the abstract mythic language of 'Autumn Equinox' in *The Wreck of the Archangel*. Similarly, rape, marriage, and widowhood follow each other in a cycle that is without a moral dimension and accepted fatalistically. In this Arcadian harmony, human beings are without choice, retaining the innocence of children in their acceptance of their harsh life:

> A winter bride is ravished with plough and seed
> And finds at last
> The crag where mother and widow enfolded stand.

Lawrence Lerner has suggested that some kinds of pastoral enact Freud's notion of wish-fulfilment. When Pope says that 'we must use some illusion to render a pastoral delightful', Lerner suggests that he was using the notion in the same way that Freud believed that 'an illusion is not the same as an error'. A wish can be projected in poetry to create an illusion that 'this is the way things really were' in an idealised nostalgia for a selectively remembered past. If the present is full of distressing 'progress', say, or demanding choices, it is possible for the writer to project a wish for the way of life perceived to be past into some rural corners of the present such as Orkney. Lerner calls this the pastoral 'poetry of illusion':

> An illusion, Freud concludes, is a belief in which 'wish-fulfilment is a prominent factor in its motivation'. The wish to find in country

life a relief from the problems of a sophisticated society formed itself, in Renaissance times, into a set of poetic conventions. These are the conventions of pastoral. Pastoral is the poetry of illusion: the Golden Age is the historiography of wish-fulfilment.

(Loughrey 1984: 154)

This is an accurate description of Mackay Brown's poetry in which it is difficult to distinguish those poems written in the voice of a child from those written in an adult voice. Only the titles indicate the difference between two poems which face each other across the pages of *The Wreck of the Archangel,* his last collection: 'Desert Sleepers' is written in exactly the same language as 'Rackwick: A Child's Scrapbook'. In the mythic innocence of this Arcadia the wish is to replace choice with the fatalism contained in what the poet calls his 'green fable' in 'Christmas Poem': 'We and earth and sun are one'. The reductiveness of this is clearly a retreat from the adult complexities of life, even in contemporary Orkney. Significantly, the one 'green' poem that Mackay Brown has written, against the drilling for uranium in Orkney in the 1970s, he tried to suppress, refusing to republish it.

In *The Deserted Village* Goldsmith describes a place he calls 'Auburn' in which he spent his youth and to which he had hoped to retire. It is an Arcadia of a childhood of 'innocence and ease', where 'decency' is the key value and is to be found even in the 'severe' schoolmaster. Just as Mackay Brown's Arcadia represents an ideal beyond Orkney and before 'Progress', Goldsmith's Arcadia in Ireland (where he grew up and where Auburn is set) represents the old English ideal revived in Morris's Utopia:

> A time there was, ere England's griefs began,
> When every rood of ground retained its man;
> For him light labour spread its wholesome store,
> Just gave what life required, but no more:

His best companions, innocence and health;
And his best riches, ignorance of wealth.

The familiar pastoral opposition of riches and wealth is also present in Mackay Brown's explanation for the depopulation of Rackwick: 'They say, the jar flawed / With heaviness of coins'. But the crucial difference is that Goldsmith's poem is a literary intervention in a precise historical moment. His 'Auburn' has been cleared of its inhabitants by enclosure and his poem is a warning to his contemporary readers. The poem continues: 'But times are altered; trade's unfeeling train / Usurp the land and dispossess the swain.' Progress is objected to, but not in an abstract generalisation; Goldsmith intervenes because the fate of the land is the fate of people:

Ill fares the land, to hastening ills a prey,
Where wealth accumulates, and men decay;
Princes and lords may flourish or may fade;
A breath can make them, as a breath has made:
But a bold peasantry, their country's pride,
When once destroy'd, can never be supplied.

This is the introduction to the poem's detailed nostalgic Arcadia and its justification. The experience of dispossession was not, of course, unknown in Scotland, but Mackay Brown does not make a single reference to the Clearances in his poetry. His Arcadia is ahistorical as well as amoral. For him 'the layers of history and culture cease to matter'. Goldsmith does idealise 'Auburn': only 'light labour' is required in his Arcadia. However, his is not a Freudian wish-fulfilment. His poem represents a wish to see a better life for the working population of the country, 'a bold peasantry' who deserve more decent treatment than enclosure and eviction. For Goldsmith, Arcadia is oppositional in function, while for Mackay Brown it is a retreat into an unchanging mythic past away from the problems of the present. But does, say, the popularity in 1969 of Ronald Blythe's supposed documentary of an East Anglian village Arcadia, *Akenfield,* represent a continuing interest in rural writing that is oppositional or escapist? The answer must lie in an understanding of the nature of pastoral retreats.

3

THE DISCOURSE
OF RETREAT

William Hazlitt, remembering the Greek and Roman origins of
the pastoral, and aware that Renaissance interest in the form
derived from Italy, did not believe that the English could be good
at writing in this mode. In 1818 Hazlitt wrote, 'We have few
good pastorals in the language. Our manners are not Arcadian;
our climate is not an eternal spring; our age is not the age of gold'
(Loughrey 1984: 73). He then went on in a characteristically
acerbic manner to dismiss, in a sentence each, the work of Sidney,
Spenser and Pope. What Hazlitt misunderstood was that the
pastoral is a retreat from 'our manners', 'our climate', 'our age', into
a literary construct. The reader recognises that the country in a
pastoral text is an Arcadia because the language is idealised. In
other words, pastoral is a discourse, a way of using language that
constructs a different kind of world from that of realism. Sidney,
Spenser and Pope may have individually distinctive styles, but they
share a discourse that creates for the reader a notion that this text
is to be read differently from those of other discourses.

Pastoral is essentially a discourse of retreat which may, as we have seen, either simply *escape* from the complexities of the city, the court, the present, 'our manners', or *explore* them. This is the difference between the pejorative and the primary senses of the pastoral, between Leo Marx's 'sentimental pastoral' and his 'complex pastoral'. That it is able to explore the present, or imagine an alternative future is only possible because the reader accepts that pastoral works as discourse. It is because retreat is a device for reflecting upon the present that the pastoral is able to 'glaunce at greater matters', as George Puttenham, writing in 1589, put it. Puttenham knew that 'the Poet devised the *Eglogue* . . . not of purpose to counterfait or represent the rusticall manner of loves and communication . . .' Despite the inclusion in shepherds' speech of elements of dialect, the pastoral tradition has been based upon an assumption that its discourse does not replicate their actual communication. Since Theocritus the pastoral has defined itself and declared itself as a literary discourse that has retreated from both the sophisticated discourse of the court and the illiterate discourse of the real shepherd. Meeting somewhere between the two, pastoral discourse is a linguistic borderland that constructs the artifice of Arcadia.

Goldsmith believed that poetry itself lived in this borderland between the peasant and the landowner, between the 'rural virtues' and the urban reader. At the end of *The Deserted Village* (1770) he imagines that if 'trade's unfeeling train' usurps not only the land, but also the values of the people in it, poetry as a discourse will die:

> And thou, sweet Poesy, thou loveliest Maid,
> Still first to fly where sensual joys invade;
> Unfit in these degenerate times of shame,
> To catch the heart, or strike for honest fame.

The moral tone of this is important because for Goldsmith the discourse of pastoral poetry has an intrinsic integrity. It may idealise, but it is fundamentally 'honest' when it is attacking the degenerate 'sensual joys' provided by the commercial exploitation of land and peasantry. If the 'rural virtues' have been banished with the inhabitants from Goldsmith's retirement retreat, what is there for poetry to celebrate?

Pastoral's celebration of retreat is its strength and its inherent weakness. When retreat is an end in itself, pastoral is merely escapist. So how much range is there in the discourse for the justifiable celebration of retreat? What diversity is there in the modes of retreat in literature that functions as pastoral? What are the achievements and weaknesses of pastoral's discourse of retreat?

James Thomson's *The Seasons*, written and revised between 1727 and 1744, celebrates everything: the country and the city, the managed agricultural land and the wastes, British countryside and the African savannah. It is the complete pastoral, idealising all these different environments in turn and, because it was written over a period in which Thomson's opinions changed, he never attempts to resolve the text's contradictions. The discourse of retreat is familiar enough:

> Oh knew he but his happiness, of men
> The happiest he! who far from public rage,
> Deep in the vale, with a choice few retir'd,
> Drinks the pure pleasures of the rural life.

But pure pleasures seem to extend throughout the land and are, in fact, not confined to secluded vales. The momentum of Thomson's discourse builds to become all-inclusive:

> Happy Britannia! where the Queen of Arts,
> Inspiring vigour, Liberty, abroad
> Walks unconfined even to thy farthest cots,
> And scatters plenty with unsparing hand.
>   Rich is thy soil, and merciful thy clime;

> Thy streams unfailing in the Summer's drought;
> Unmatched thy guardian-oaks; thy valleys float
> With golden waves; and on thy mountains flocks
> Bleat numberless; while, roving round their sides,
> Bellow the blackening herds in lusty droves.
> Beneath, thy meadows glow, and rise unquelled
> Against the mower's sythe. On every hand
> Thy villas shine. Thy country teems with wealth;
> And Property assures it to the swain,
> Pleased and unwearied in his guarded toil.

It is hard to realise that Thomson is actually describing the same country in the same century as Goldsmith, but Thomson is, of course, describing a landowner's vision of what follows from enclosure. From his shining new country house the man of property distributes the country's wealth to the single remaining swain who has laboured to produce it. His work is now 'guarded toil' – that is guarded by his master – Thomson goes out of his way to point out in a later revision of what was originally 'certain toil'. The poem goes on to celebrate the city where the sweating figure of Drudgery manages to 'look gay', just as his country brother is 'pleased and unwearied' in his work. Indeed, in 'Autumn' Thomson describes the city as the key development in the growth of civilisation:

> Nurse of art, the city reared
> In beauteous pride her tower-encircled head;
> And, stretching street to street, by thousands drew,
> From twining woody haunts, or the tough yew
> To bows strong-straining, her aspiring sons.

The pleasures of rural life 'deep in the vale' have become, here, the 'twining woody haunts' of the uncivilised. Thomson simply accepts that he feels a contradictory tension between the awesome fecundity of raw nature, especially in Africa, and what he feels can be achieved by the commercial management of those forces. On the one hand Africa represents the Golden Age 'yet undisturbed / By Christian crimes and Europe's cruel sons', where corn grows without the sweat of labour – 'Ceres void of pain'; on the other hand he immediately asks, without a humanising presence 'what avails this wondrous waste of wealth'? At bottom, Thomson's ambivalence towards raw nature is driven by an Augustan fascination and fear that strikes at the heart of a perception of human nature: in humans raw nature is raw passion, as it probably is, Thomson suspects, in Africa:

> Love dwells not there,
> The soft regards, the tenderness of life,
> The heart-shed tear, the ineffable delight
> Of sweet humanity: these court the beam
> Of milder climes – in selfish fierce desire
> And the wild fury of voluptuous sense
> There lost.

So Thomson's pastoral is ultimately a retreat from 'fierce desire' which would inevitably be as 'selfish' as it would be 'voluptuous'. This is what the cultivation of nature in the land represents to the Augustans: the restraining 'cultivation' – the word now takes on its full cultural meaning – of human nature. It's just that the resulting 'tenderness of life' is not extended to sweating 'Drudgery himself' who actually does the cultivation of the land.

But, as Raymond Williams pointed out, there is a parallel reversal in a shifting of praise in the text from the 'power of cultivation' to 'the desolate prospect' that 'thrills the soul' (Williams 1975: 91) where 'the power / Of philosophic Melancholy comes'. Here Thomson is anticipating the discourse of retreat of the late eighteenth century in which pastoral represents an alternative experience of lonely melancholy. Here is the retreat to an emotional state that is safely opposed to 'fierce desire'. In Gray's 'Elegy Written in a Country Churchyard' (1750) pastoral celebrates the ultimate retreat. This is the defining poem of the discourse of retreat towards deathliness. It is set in that crepuscular borderland between the living and the dead, and sensuously displays the imagery of the Gothic:

> Now fades the glimmering landscape on the sight,
> And all the air a solemn stillness holds,
> Save where the beetle wheels his droning flight,
> And drowsy tinklings lull the distant folds;
>
> Save that from yonder ivy-mantled tow'r
> The mopeing owl does to the moon complain
> Of such, as wond'ring near her secret bow'r,
> Molest her ancient solitary reign.
>
> Beneath those rugged elms, that yew-tree's shade,
> Where heaves the turf in many a mould'ring heap,
> Each in his narrow cell for ever laid,
> The rude Forefathers of the hamlet sleep.

Beetle, owl, ivy, moon: the icons lead inevitably to the dead, who far from sleeping, are heaving under the unfortunately still 'mould'ring' turf to appear, as indeed they eventually do, 'at the peep of dawn'. But this discourse serves a moral purpose:

> Let not Ambition mock their useful toil,
> Their homely joys, and destiny obscure;
> Nor Grandeur hear with a disdainful smile,
> The short and simple annals of the poor.

Against 'the simple annals of the poor' are set not only 'Ambition', but 'Luxury and Pride' – in fact, 'all that wealth e'er gave'. This is familiar criticism of the urban values of 'the madding crowd's ignoble strife'. What is significant is that the real country worker who is invisible in the Eden of Pope's 'Epistles', whose 'rudeness' is tolerated in Ben Jonson's Arcadias, who is accepted as the necessary, but happy, labour of improved agriculture in Thomson's *The Seasons*, is now idealised precisely because poverty prevents rebellion. Ironically the poem accumulates plenty of reasons for resentment:

> Perhaps in this neglected spot is laid
> Some heart once pregnant with celestial fire;
> Hands, that the rod of empire might have sway'd,
> Or wak'd to extasy the living lyre.
>
> But Knowledge to their eyes her ample page
> Rich with the spoils of time did ne'er unroll;
> Chill Penury repress'd their noble rage,
> And froze the genial current of the soul.

'Chill Penury' is real poverty, rather than the joyful versions of it so far seen in pastoral discourse. And yet Thomas Gray's indulgence in melancholy turns even the poor's inability, through 'Chill Penury' itself, to express their resentment into an idealised virtue: the poor are too busy coping with poverty and thus suppress their anger with an admirable restraint. The suggestion that their justifiable rage is 'noble' rings a little hollow in this context. When Thomson says 'Some mute inglorious Milton here may rest', he is not actually regretting the loss of this peasant poet, but praising the poor for accepting their loss. To be 'inglorious' is more important in his scale of values, because it is tinged with the sadness of being mute. The result of Gray's retreat is to exploit the country poor for his melancholy, whilst appearing to celebrate their dignity. His patronising notion of dignity is that they have accepted their lot:

> Far from the madding crowd's ignoble strife,
> Their sober wishes never learn'd to stray;
> Along the cool sequester'd vale of life
> They kept the noiseless tenor of their way.

One can see why pastorals of this kind were used for the education of the masses in anthologies of poetry for the classrooms of the British Empire. The future clerks of the colonial bureaucracy had to be taught, like colonial subjects, that 'their sober wishes never learn'd to stray'.

There is a sense in which the English pastoral has always been able to make criticisms of the establishment, whilst at the same time warning against a radical disturbance of the social order. This is the double edge of the critique of avarice. The retreat from the urban world of court and commerce, where riches are valued, not only provides an opportunity for criticising material values, but implies that others should not aspire to them. Spenser's more earthy pastoral *The Shepheardes Calendar* (1579), often regarded as the first important pastoral in English, is an interesting example of this double function because it is expressed in what would now be called an ecological conception of nature.

Unlike Spenser's *Astrophel* (1586) or *The Faerie Queene* (1595), which were discussed in the previous chapter, the poet attempts a discourse closer to realism in the shepherds of this earlier pastoral. In the 'May' section we are told that it is, in fact, the experience of idealisation itself that,

> Lulled the shepheards in such securitie,
> That not content with loyall obeysaunce,
> Some gan to gape for greedie governaunce,
> And match them selfe with mighty potentates,
> Lovers of Lordship and troublers of states.

This speech is given to the shepherd Piers who knows that while he can imply to his court audience that 'Lovers of Lordship' might be 'troublers of states', the role of a shepherd is not to be questioned. He continues,

> Tho gan shepheards swaines to looke a loft,
> And leave to live hard, and learn to ligge soft:
> Tho under colour of shepeheards, somewhile
> There crept in Wolves, ful of fraude and guile,
> That often devoured their owne sheepe,
> And often the shepheards, that did hem keepe.

The allegorical moral here is clear for Spenser's literate-class readers: those who would be upwardly mobile ('looke a loft') and desire to lie in softer beds ('ligge soft') can find themselves manipulated by ambitious wolves who will eat them up as well as their source of income.

The rationale underpinning the social order of *The Shepheardes Calendar* is established in the amusing dialogue between the old shepherd, Thenot and the dissatisfied 'laesie laddie', Cuddie, in the 'February' section. First it is the conditions of winter that Cuddie complains about in a vigorous form of verse that gains authenticity from its dialect ('gryde' means 'pierced', and 'rontes' are bullocks):

> Ah for pittie, wil rancke Winters rage,
> These bitter blasts never ginne tasswage?
> The kene cold blowes through my beaten hyde,
> All as I were through the body gryde.
> My ragged rontes all shiver and shake,
> As doen high Towers in an earthquake:
> They wont in the wind wagge their wrigle tailes,
> Perke as Peacock: but nowe it avales.

This appears to be a conscious imitation of the language of the two herdsmen, Battus and Corydon, in the *Idylls* of Theocritus. Here, of course, the complaint is not about the ground being 'one thorny ambush', but about an English winter. Thenot, however, has a more sophisticated argument for cheering up Cuddie than Corydon's 'the dawn is always new' to Battus:

> Lewdly complainest thou laesie ladde,
> Of Winters wracke, for making thee sadde.
> Must not the world wend in his commun course
> From good to badd, and from badde to worse,
> From worse unto that is worst of all,
> And then returne to his former fall?

This is not the best of news for Cuddie, but it is at least based upon an understanding of the cycles of nature and an assumption that human beings are part of the world's 'commun course'.

Thenot goes on to elaborate a stoical philosophy that has clear social implications:

> Selfe have I worne out thrise threttie yeares,
> Some in much joy, many in many teares:
> Yet never complained of cold nor heate,
> Of Sommers flame, nor of Winters threat:
> Ne ever was to Fortune foeman,
> But gentle tooke, that ungently came.
> And ever my flocke was my chief care,
> Winter or Sommer they mought well fare.

Thenot accepts what comes, does not want to challenge fortune, and considers only the work he is born to. Pastoral retreat is a return to essentials; it is reductive in a way that can be either simplistic or profound. This is not a matter of the discourse itself having simplicity or complexity in its use of language. Elaborate poetics can express simplistic notions, just as Lear's repetition of 'never, never, never, never' at the end of *King Lear* is one of Shakespeare's most profound effects. It is a matter of the discourse recognising the necessary qualifications, reservations, contextualities any expression of essentials must contain. Thenot begins by being simplistic in his vision, but ends with some degree of environmental and philosophical profundity.

Actually, like Battus, Cuddie's dissatisfaction is really the result of love. Thenot knows that Cuddie will not listen to his lectures about youth as 'a bubble blown up with breath', so he offers to tell him 'a tale of truth'. The allegory that ensues is about an old oak beside which grows 'a bragging brere'. The briar complains to the farmer that the shade of the oak is inhibiting his own growth, but when the farmer cuts the oak down, the briar, although 'puffed up with pryde and vaine pleasaunce' at first, has not thought about the winter:

> For eftsones Winter gan to approche,
> The blustring Boreas did encroche,
> And beate upon the solitarie Brere:
> For nowe no succoure was seene him nere.

Frost, rain and snow knock him down and the feet of cattle do the rest. 'Such was thend of this Ambitious brere, / For scorning Eld.'

This final moral gives the story the effect of a fable: this is what happens to the ambitious who scorn the wisdom of their elders. But this is an abrupt addition. The force of the narrative lies elsewhere, in the ecological relationship that the briar has with the old oak. Spenser invests the oak with religious significance – 'Sacred with many a mysteree' – and critics differ in their interpretations of Spenser's purpose here, Helen Cooper suggesting that this may be 'an allegory of the history of the Church (Cooper 1977: 157), while Barrell and Bull detect 'an anti-clerical satire' (Barrell and Bull 1974: 35). However, the oak does not need to be sacred for the narrative to make its point in favour of a pluralist tolerance. The natural symbiotic dependency of the briar on the oak endorses not only the integrity of each species, but an interdependence that is not always obvious. This is the ideology that underpins Thenot's stoicism. That there is a difference between shepherd and courtier is only another aspect of nature's diversity and both need this difference to be maintained as part of the natural order. The court needs the shepherd to be a shepherd as much as the shepherd needs the court to rule him. Unfortunately all this is lost on Cuddie:

> Here is a long tale, and little worth.
> So long have I listened to thy speche,
> That graffed to the ground is my breche.

Such graphically realistic discourse as this in *The Shepheardes Calendar* is rarely to be found in the Elizabethan pastoral dramas that emerged out of court activities such as 'Maying' and the Revels, although echoes of the Elizabethan poet Spenser might be found in the occasional use of his characters and his love plots. George Peele's play *The Arraignment of Paris* (1581), for example, contained a pastoral episode with a love-lorn Colin and a Thenot that is borrowed directly from *The Shepheardes Calendar*. But Elizabeth, like her court, preferred to meet her shepherds in a context carrying several levels of retreat from the discourse of reality. In 1592, at the Entertainment at Sudeley, 'an old shepherd' greeted the Queen in a language as courtly as it was reassuring:

> Vouchsafe to hear a simple shepherd: shepherds and simplicity cannot part. Your Highness is come into Cotshold, an uneven country, but a people that carry their thoughts level with their fortunes; low spirits, but true hearts, using plain dealing, once counted a jewel, now beggary. These hills afford nothing but cottages and nothing can we present unto your Highness but shepherds; the country healthy and harmless; a fresh air where there are no damps, and where a black sheep is a

perilous beast; no monsters. We carry our hearts at our
tongues' ends, being as far from dissembling as our sheep from
fierceness.

(Hunter 1962: 130)

That this shepherd's statement reassuring the Queen that the
country is 'harmless' is believed to have been written by the court
playwright, John Lyly, indicates just how dissembling this
language actually is. Using alliteration, witty repetition, inventive
imagery and a clinching simile, this 'simple old shepherd' eloquently tells the Queen that her retreat into the Cotswolds is to
be as unthreatening as it is far from the fierceness of court intrigue,
'free', indeed, 'from sad cares that rich men's hearts devour'
(Hunter 1962: 130).

   John Lyly's pastoral play *Gallathea* is based upon the sixth idyll
of Theocritus in which the monster Polyphemus attempts to
seduce the nymph Galatea. Lyly's monster, the Agar, however,
seems to be named from the 'eagre' which is the tidal wave of
the Humber estuary. For Lyly has transposed the heat of classical
Greece to his native Lincolnshire with surprising results, as the
opening words of the play indicate:

The sun doth beat upon the plain fields; wherefore let us sit
down, Gallathea, under this fair oak, by whose broad leaves
being defended from the warm beams we may enjoy the fresh
air which softly breathes from Humber floods.

(Hunter 1962: 194)

Many contemporary Lincolnshire nymphs, the successors to Lyly's
'passing fair maids', will perhaps recognise this as a place where the
classic battle between Diana and Cupid is still acted out. At the
centre of the Elizabethan pastoral is the tension between chastity
(Diana) and desire (Cupid), loyalty and deceit, obedience and
deception, fate and choice, eloquent denial and coarse animal lust,

courtly love and the rape of the monster. To attempt to deceive the gods by giving way to Cupid's arrows is to risk a retribution that can even extend to the land itself. The narrative with which the play opens sets the theme by suggesting that 'sacrilege' and 'rebellion' (the social here symbolising the emotional) can have apocryphal results, as witnessed by this remarkable threat of the flooding of the Lincolnshire fens:

> But Fortune, constant in nothing but inconstancy, did change her copy, as the people their custom; for the land being oppressed by Danes, who instead of sacrifice committed sacrilege, instead of religion, rebellion; and made a prey of that in which they should have made their prayers, tearing down the temple even with the earth, being almost equal with the skies; enraged so the god who binds the winds in the hollows of the earth that he caused the seas to break their bounds, sith men had broke their vows, and to swell as far above their reach as men had swerved beyond their reason. Then might you see ships sail where sheep fed, anchors cast where ploughs go, fishermen throw their nets where husbandmen sow their corn, and fishes throw their scales where fowls do breed their quills. Then might you gather froth where now is dew, rotten weeds for sweet roses, and take view of monstrous mermaids instead of passing fair maids.
>
> (Hunter 1962: 196)

In the same language of the 'old shepherd', Lyly delights in alliterative contrasts to demonstrate that if people 'change their custom' their very environment is threatened with radical change. 'Froth' and 'rotten weeds', those Elizabethan images of personal and social corruption, will accompany the change of fair maids into monsters. The breaking of bounds in personal behaviour, as in the rape and pillage committed by the Vikings, will result in the very sea breaking its bounds in the fragile borderland of earth and sea that is the Lincolnshire coast. Although no courtiers appear in *Gallathea*, the implications for courtiers on a personal and a political level are as clear as are the implications for shepherds who might want to pretend to be 'gentlemen born', like the *nouveau riche* shepherds at the end of Shakespeare's *The Winter's Tale* (1611). To a court in which the newfound wealth of merchants was producing an aspiring capitalist class in whom grace, honour and loyalty had not been bred in the traditional aristocratic dynasty, the discourse of pastoral retreat served to warn those who might be tempted to challenge their destiny. The spectre of civil war, that dominant and growing Elizabethan horror, lurks below the surface of the pastoral drama just as powerfully as it is explicit in Shakespeare's history plays. The function of pastoral retreat, where the conflicting temptations of honour and desire in love can be explored in the safe arena of classical stability, is very much to remind the courtier audience that, as Gallathea says to her father in the first scene, 'Destiny may be deferred, not prevented.' Honour and political desire that might challenge the destiny of the fixed order, is the subtext of the pastoral drama.

It might therefore seem that the subversive hero Robin Hood would be an inappropriate figure to invoke in the prologue to a pastoral as Ben Jonson does in his play *The Sad Shepherd* (1612). But he can do so knowing that the mythic hero is a safe distance in rustic simplicity from the sophisticated mode of political subversion his audience might be tempted to desire. In fact, the call of Robin to shepherds and shepherdesses of the Vale of Be'voir to a feast in Sherwood Forest locates Jonson's pastoral retreat in the heart of English rather than classical Arcadia. Despite Jonson's address to the 'Critick' and references to the 'Muses hill', his courtly wit is in tension with an apparent desire for a certain element of realism. His sad shepherd has lost his lover in the Trent and his shepherds are dispirited by a recent cultural change (in 1612 when it was first performed) that has undercut, with Puritan disdain, their traditional sports as 'pagan pastimes':

> They call ours, Pagan pastimes, that infect
> Our blood with ease, our youth with all neglect,
> Our tongues with wantonness, our thoughts with lust.

Robin reveals that the purpose of Jonson's retreat is to comment upon those Puritanical trends that led Shakespeare to write *Measure for Measure* and Jonson to rhyme 'mistrust' with 'lust' as though one led to the other: 'Those charitable times had no mistrust. / Shepherds knew how to love, and not to lust.'

If Jonson's retreat is into a nostalgia for an English pre-Puritan Arcadia, Samuel Daniel's drama *The Queenes Arcadia* (1606) begins with the complaint that this classical Arcadia is suffering from,

> So universall a distemperature,
> In all parts of the body of our state . . .
> Our ancient Pastorall habits are despis'd
> And all is strange, hearts, clothes, and all disguis'd.

The signs of social change are registered in Daniel's retreat, but the finger is not pointed at Puritanism. The purpose of this Arcadia is to demonstrate how the stability of the Queen's court is threatened by a new generation of negotiators such as the lawyer Lincus who complains that,

> These poore people of Arcadia here
> Are soone contented each man with his owne,
> As they desire no more, nor will be drawne
> To any contestation.

The Elizabethan society of 1606 is shown to be one in which a lawyer is now as indispensable as his work is absent from Daniel's ironically named *The Queenes Arcadia* where there are,

> No puchasings, no contracts, no comerse,
> No politique commands, no services,
> No generall assemblies but to feast,
> And to delight themselves with fresh pastimes.

The lawyer's lament is wittily touching and heartfelt: 'How can I hope that ever I shall thrive?'

This discourse is so obviously an ironic reflection back at the audience that it is easy to forget that the central conceit and concern of Renaissance pastorals is with personal choices in love. Economic realities do intrude in the most unexpected places such as the extended love song that is Michael Drayton's play *The Shepheard's Sirena* (1627). Most of this pastoral is an Elizabethan delight in such lines as:

> All thy Sands silver Trent
> > Downe to the Humber,
> The sighes that I have spent
> > never can number.

Dorilus's sighs have been for Sirena's apparent hibernation indoors for the winter, since she lives by the 'silver Trent', which sums up the amusing contradictions that arise from a classical pastoral set in an English Arcadia. Yet at the end, Dorilus chooses, under severe pressure from his mocking friends, to take up his sheephook and defend the pastures against the new fashion for unlyrical 'Rougish Swineherds' whose pigs will 'wroote up all our Downes'. That Drayton was unsuccessful in seeking patronage in the Elizabethan court is perhaps not surprising in view of his inability to integrate artistically his classical/English Arcadian location, the conflicting demands of languishing love and the need to preserve a livelihood against threatening swineherds. Here the borderlands of pastoral retreat are so separate that they render the pastoral enterprise absurd.

Perhaps the starkest example of Renaissance drama's search for a pastoral retreat in which to locate choices in love is John Fletcher's *The Faithfull Shepheardesse* (1610). His sources are an indication of the range of pastoral influences available to a Stuart playwright. Lawrence B. Wallis suggests the classical unities of the Italian High Renaissance pastoral drama such as Guarini's *Il Pastor Fido*, characters from *The Shepheardes Calendar*, the theme of chastity from the third book of *The Faerie Queene*, the romance plot from the recent success of Shakespeare's *Pericles* and some of the poetry of *A Midsummer Night's Dream* (Wallis 1968: 186–8). The fact that the latter two have no literal pastoral elements does not negate their influence on a dramatist who also wrote plays other than pastorals.

The discourse of these servants of Pan is polarised between, on the one hand, 'the fit of lust' that enables Cloe to declare, 'It is impossible to ravish me, / I am so willing', a state achieved by two women and one 'sullen shepherd' (which this play attributes to 'the high rebellious heat / Of grapes, and strength of meat'), and on the other hand, a chastity that keeps the shepherdess of the title, Clorin, a virgin who is conveniently in love with a dead lover. The Victorian critic W. W. Greg was so shocked that he could perceive no development in the play, whilst, in the next generation of critics, Una Ellis-Fermor concluded, when considering this play, that 'chastity, like the player-queen, doth protest too much' (Wallis 1968: 188–9).

Although there is a reference to 'the many neighbouring towns', this pastoral is firmly set in the meads, downs and woods of a pagan Greece. At one point the lust-crazed Sullen Shepherd, the monster of this pastoral, is described as the corrupter of this society, but the simile serves to indicate that this is a play about personal choice rather than a corrupt state:

> Monster, stay!
> Thou art like a canker to the state

Thou liv'st and breat'st in, eating with debate
Through every honest bosom.

This debate is what the play conducts and tests by the interaction of representative characters. Perigot is the male equivalent of Clorin. In the night of the play he lies down in the wood adjacent to, if not exactly beside his lover, but tries to kill her when he thinks she is interested in sex. In fact, he wounds the shepherdess who would be his lover. When he then meets his original lover, Amoret, they debate the way in which chastity keeps them from their animal selves:

> *Perigot*:   Men ever were most blessed, till cross fate
>   Brought love and woman forth, unfortunate
>   To all that ever tasted of their smiles;
>   Whose actions are all double, full of wiles;
>   Like to the subtle hare, that 'fore the hounds
>   Makes many turnings, leaps and many rounds,
>   This way and that way, to deceive the scent
>   Of her pursuers.
>
> *Amoret*:   'Tis but to prevent
>   Their speedy coming on, that seek her fall;
>   The hands of cruel men, more bestial,
>   And of a nature more refusing good
>   Than the beasts themselves or fishes of the flood.

What is remarkable about this is its even-handed treatment of the fear – the deep Renaissance anxiety – of each gender's ability to lose the sophistication of language and art at the very moment of achieving what art has been used to pursue. When compassion and moderation have been arrived at in the play, it is by a healing process that has come from reflecting upon the destructive consequences of aggressive 'appetite'. Clorin declares, 'What art could not have cured is healed by wit.'

But to get to that stage a little pagan magic has been necessary. Amoret, who was disposed of by being thrown down a well in the heat of the action, is brought up again by the God of the River who lives in the stream that is its source. At the heart of this play, in the absence of a sense of the state and its potential political instability, is a sense of the natural environment that is both the negative source of the animal passions that drive the play and the positive 'fountain' of life, however problematic that might be. The two long speeches of the God of the River remind listeners of both their connectedness and their separation from the natural forces in which they have their home. The location of this retreat in pagan Greece provides a distance from which to view this disturbing idea. When Amoret offers thanks to this 'Immortal power that rul'st this holy flood', the God reminds her that his 'neighbour-people', having respected the power of the river by sacrificing two lambs, will not this year have their economic livelihoods ruined by his sacred power:

For which this year they shall be free
From raging floods, that as they pass
Leave their gravel in the grass;
Nor shall their meads be overflown
When their grass is newly mown.

Such crucial detail betrays a respect on the part of the playwright himself for the power of a river, and he gives Amoret a speech in response which draws upon the respect of one who has seen the damage that can be done by careless users of rivers:

For thy kindness to me shown
Never from thy banks be blown
Any tree, with windy force,
Cross thy streams, to stop thy course;
May no beast that comes to drink,

> With his horns cast down thy brink;
> May none that for thy fish do look,
> Cut thy banks to dam thy brook;
> Barefoot may no neighbour wade
> In thy cool streams, wife nor maid,
> When the spawns on stones do lie,
> To wash their hemp, and spoil the fry!

It is no accident that this discourse of a respectful relationship with a river echoes the moral tenure of the play's treatment of the animal force in human relationships. All this river discourse is a healing allegory at the turning point of the plot's dramatic dialectic between lust and chastity. Amoret's ecocentric speech sets the tone for a less egocentric attitude in characters such as Alexis who comes to say,

> I have forgot all vain desires,
> All looser thoughts, ill-tempered fires:
> True love I find a pleasant fume,
> Whose moderate heat can ne'er consume.

Whilst 'moderate heat' does now give recognition to that animal 'heat', unlike the extreme of chastity, it also seems that chastity, as Clorin comes to see, need only be a necessary temporary state 'unless the faithful love / Of some good shepherd force thee to remove' from a 'virgin-state', in which case fidelity supersedes chastity. When Clorin finally advises, 'Be famous for your good, not for your crime', one is reminded that the crime against inner nature's forces that set the play in motion began with a parody of a popular Renaissance court pastime by Fletcher's having everyone who entered eloquently declaring their love for the previous person. The very discourse of escape has again held a mirror to the contemporary audience.

One of those mirrors in Renaissance drama reflected notions of sexuality which, whilst often appearing to endorse the male view of the female as both dangerously mysterious and in need of male protection, could also challenge these assumptions within the borderland of pastoral retreat, as can be seen in the range of sexual behaviours in *The Faithfull Shepheardesse*. In a forthcoming book Karoline Szatek will show that critics have been too casual in their classification of sexuality in these dramas. She argues that 'sanctioned ideologies regarding human sexuality become intersected with alternative ones in the shaded space of the pastoral borderland, providing an area where authors can point out other, perhaps more appropriate, views on female sexuality, explore notions of cross-dressing, and examine the realm of alternative sexual relationships' (Szatek 1995: 94). Szatek points to Thomas Lodge's *Rosalynde* (1590), the basis for Shakespeare's *As You Like It*, as an example of the expansion of notions of the female and an exploration through the eroticism of cross-dressing of alternative sexualities. The key point here is that 'in the shaded space of the pastoral borderland' sexuality can be explored rather than offered with the full threatening force of revolutionary alternatives.

It is Shakespeare whose pastoral dramas can take an audience into Arden or Bohemia to examine the relationships between notions of male and female, the personal and the political, lust and love, honour and deception, human nature and 'great creating nature' with a density of a different order. But he explicitly completes the cycle of return to the court rather than hold up his retreat as an ironic mirror. His pastorals will therefore be discussed in the following chapter.

The Elizabethan Golden Age of discovery and commerce, which had renewed an interest in both classical pastoral's Golden Age and the contemporary Italian pastoral drama, gave way in the seventeenth century to a mode of pastoral retreat that was able to bring together a sense of ownership of the contemporary location of retreat (in the country-house Arcadias discussed in the previous chapter), a metaphorical treatment of the new frontiers of science, rationalism and colonisation, together with a concern for personal salvation in increasingly Puritan terms. The perfect location for seventeenth-century pastoral retreat was the garden. The way this motif was used by Milton, after pastoral forays in *Lycidas* (1637) and *L'Allegro* (written 1632), in *Paradise Lost* (1667) and by Marvell in several metaphysical poems might provide a contrast in the limitations and achievements of the process of retreat. Some of the potential problems can be anticipated in Milton's two earlier works.

Dr Johnson was characteristically sceptical about a 'species of poetry' that was an escape from 'cares and perturbations' into 'Elysian regions, where we are to meet with nothing but joy, and plenty and contentment; where every gale whispers pleasure, and every shade promises repose' (Blunden 1929: 89). He was particularly irritated by Milton's *Lycidas*, a lament for a drowned classical shepherd who is announced in an epigraph to be actually 'a learned Friend, unfortunately drown'd in his Passage from Chester on the Irish Seas, 1637'. Johnson finds grief for a real friend ringing hollow in the tired imagery of melancholy myrtle and ivy that Milton had already exhausted in *L'Allegro*. These shepherds, Johnson says, are as unconvincing in their passion as they are in their vague statements about what they do:

> We know that they never drove a field, and that they had no flocks to batten; and although it be allowed that the representation may be allegorical, the true meaning is so uncertain and remote, that it is never sought, because it cannot be known when it is found.
>
> (Loughrey 1984: 71)

Even allowing for Johnson's delight in his rhetoric of attack, he has a point. Milton's real purpose in *Lycidas* is also declared in the epigraph: it 'by occasion fortels the ruine of our corrupted Clergy then in their height'. The reasons for retreat are therefore confused in the poem's conception.

By contrast Tennyson's lament for Arthur Hallam, *In Memoriam* (1850), which follows 'my Arthur', as Tennyson calls him, in his occasional retreat from the town into both garden and 'the landscape winking thro' the heat', is convincing not only because of the sensuous Tennysonian detail, but because it is underpinned with Man's darker, more difficult knowledge:

> Who trusted God was love indeed
>   And love Creation's final law –
>   Tho' Nature, red in tooth and claw
> With ravine, shriek'd against his creed.

This is a nature entirely absent from Milton's garden of Eden in Book IV of *Paradise Lost*. That nature, Creation itself, might contain both predator and progenitor, the drive towards death and the impulse towards love, which must both be recognised and accepted in a complex theology, is hardly suggested by Milton's image of Satan sitting like a cormorant on the Tree of Life. For Milton's focus is on moral choice, 'Knowledge of Good bought dear by knowing ill', and his garden is more of a testing ground, a retreat that is both a celebration of the order of Creation and a seduction in its luxurious Arcadian discourse. For Milton the Fall is ironically a result of an innocent enjoyment of the garden's fecundity that ignores the Serpent, who, it turns out, is the incarnation of that Renaissance revulsion and fascination for 'appetite', sexual desire. In an amazing development in Book IX, Milton compares the Serpent's homing in on Eve with the way the delights of the country after an escape from the town can be crystallised in the appearance of a country girl:

> As one who long in populous City pent,
> Where Houses thick and Sewers annoy the Aire,
> Forth issuing on a Summers Morn to breathe
> Among the pleasant Villages and Farmes

Adjoind, from each thing met conceaves delight,
The smell of Grain, or tedded Grass, or Kine,
Or Daire, each rural sight, each rural sound;
If chance with Nymphlike step fair Virgin pass,
What pleasing seemd, for her now pleases more,
Shee most, and in her look summs all Delight.

When one remembers that this is supposedly the Serpent's view, one realises the problem Milton himself has with the seductions of rural retreat and a sensuality that leads to sexuality. The movement from the urban smell of sewers, to the smells, sights and sounds of nature that are 'summed' in the look of the 'fair Virgin', is both sensually persuasive and morally suspect in that the girl, like Milton's Garden of Eden itself, is a beautiful victim.

If it is Coleridge who comes to confront the difficulties of the Serpent, it is Marvell who explores the contradictions of the garden most thoroughly and thoughtfully. In his poem 'The Mower against Gardens' (1681), Marvell has his mower ridicule the absurdity of enclosing and nurturing wild Nature: ''Tis all enforc'd; the Fountain and the Grot; / While the sweet Fields do lye forgot'. A leisure versus work ethic is introduced here to deepen the unnatural/natural dichotomy. This added tension is developed into an attack on the pastoral itself: 'And Fauns and Fairyes do the Meadows till, / More by their presence than their skill.' Yet the extremity of this wit hints that Marvell himself is not entirely endorsing his Mower. 'Grafting upon the Wild the Tame', against which the Mower complains, is clearly at the centre of the burgeoning colonial enterprise of the seventeenth century. The Puritan colonisers of Marvell's poem 'Bermudas' (1681) may be praising the way wild nature seems to be providing for them, but the absurdity of their discourse betrays their rapacious intent towards what God has provided: 'He makes the Figs our mouths to meet; / And throws the Melons at our feet.' The job of exploiting nature, taming the wild, converting the innocent, is about to begin, as Marvell hints at the end of 'Bermudas' when he steps back from the Puritans' song of praise in his framing quatrain which ironically draws attention to the 'holiness' of the enterprise and the essential sense of order that drives it:

> Thus sang they, in the English boat,
> An holy and a chearful Note,
> And all the way, to guide their Chime,
> With falling Oars they kept the time.

In 'The Garden' (1681) Marvell finds a way of integrating these tensions as the garden becomes a metaphor for integrating passion, mind and soul in an image of order that resolves the human relationship with the natural.

> When we have run our Passions heat,
> Love hither makes his best retreat.
> The Gods, that mortal Beauty chase,
> Still in a Tree did end their race.

That an intelligence as active and complex as Marvell's can come to commend the contemplation of a tree in order to still the intensity of passion is as remarkable as it is profound. For Marvell's insight is that human passion and, indeed, the human mind, are a source of natural fecundity with which we can understand the continuity of our inner nature with outer nature. The imagination, combining feeling, thought and soul, can learn from a tree, or 'th' industrious bee', to see into the heart of creation:

> The Mind, that Ocean where each kind
> Does streight its own resemblance find;
> Yet it creates, transcending these,
> Far other Worlds, and other Seas;
> Annihilating all that's made
> To a green Thought in a green Shade.

This represents one of the deepest achievements of a discourse of retreat because it integrates and distils, within the context of the whole poem, so many different and contradictory elements. At the very moment that the language is celebrating the mind's capacity for both 'resemblance' and transcendence, its paradoxical ability to narrow down and apprehend the source of the natural world is offered with humility. In the shade of the garden, thought can both focus on the 'green' of a tree, say, and recognise that it is itself 'green'. In this Marvell is perhaps anticipating Wordsworth's discovery of how 'exquisitely the individual Mind . . . to the external world / Is fitted' and the contemporary American poet Gary Snyder's notion of the mind as 'wild' and language as 'a wild ecosystem' (Snyder 1995: 168).

But retreat can also offer a temptation to disconnection, an escapism from complexity and contradiction. The contemporary sense of pastoral as a pejorative term perhaps resides in the Georgian poets' lasting effect upon English culture. Between 1912 and 1922 Edward Marsh edited five anthologies of *Georgian Poetry* containing poems by Rupert Brooke, A. E. Houseman, W. H. Davies, John Masefield, Walter de la Mare, Edmund Blunden and others. Following the horrors of the First World War, these poets sought refuge in rural images that did not disturb a sense of comfortable reassurance. They only wanted time, as W. H. Davies put it, to 'stand and stare' from a gate, their minds largely disengaged. When, in a book on *Nature in Literature* (1929), Edmund Blunden quoted Dr Johnson's criticism of pastoral as a retreat into 'Elysian regions where we are to meet with nothing but joy', Blunden replied, 'And why not? Must that word "stark" be always ringing in our ears?' One has only to think of Coleridge's demand in *The Rime of the Ancient Mariner* (1798) that the water snakes, Coleridge's Serpent image, be not only recognised but blessed, to realise how far away the Georgians were from a full engagement with the natural world. Coleridge's preoccupation with the darker presences of his mind, knowing that they had their reality in external nature, prevented him from being a pastoralist in the pejorative sense. Whilst the Georgians, on the other hand, established in English culture a discourse of escape into rural reassurance that continues today with *The Archers* and the *Guardian's* daily County Diary.

Of course, the Georgian poets did not spring forth to meet the needs of their times in a literary vacuum. During the nineteenth century a tradition of rural observers had been growing, many of whom were also novelists (although their novels are sometimes hard to distinguish from their nature essays), whose cultural function was to reconnect their newly urbanised readership with the countryside they or their family had recently left behind. In 1800 nearly two-thirds of the population of England lived in rural areas, but the 1901 census showed that 77 per cent of the population then lived in urban areas and only 12 per cent of males were employed in agricultural work. The impulse behind the appetite for rural poetry, non-fiction and novels around the turn of the century is not only nostalgia, but also, as Jeremy Hooker says of Richard Jefferies's novel *After London* (1885), the wider crisis of modernity and modernism's challenge to Victorian values. As the cry of 'Make it new!' followed the disturbance of Darwinism, and E. M. Forster's 'Everything exists, nothing has value' followed Hardy's complaint against 'The President of the Immortals', Georgian retreat or the full-blown Nature worship of the novels of John Cooper Powys seemed an attractive alternative, opposition even, to the turmoil of the times, as pastoral had been before.

W. J. Keith is the leading scholar on what he calls 'non-fiction prose writers'. In America they would be called 'nature writers' and this is the term I prefer to use for our contemporaries like William Condry and Richard Mabey, whose prose quality is itself a source of enlightenment as much as the equally valuable content of a writer 'about nature' such as Oliver Rackham. Keith's historical sequence of authors is a revelation of the variety of kinds of writing about nature, countryside, landscape, natural history – these constructions also reveal the difficulties of distinctions here – that give glimpses of retreat: Izaak Walton's *The Compleat Angler* (1653), a georgic that implies a classic pastoral distinction between the simple country and the complicated town; Gilbert White's *The Natural History of Selborne* (1789) now appears in American books as the original nature writing, a natural history in which 'a natural history of the people of his day', as Richard Jefferies complained, is as absent as any awareness of Gray's 'Chill Penury'; William Cobbett, whose *Rural Rides* (1830) remains a strangely moving down-to-earth documentation of the causes of 'Chill Penury' in the failure of small farms in the early nineteenth century; Mary Russell Mitford, whose interest in offering, in her own words 'a pretty picture', tended to narrow to a fine account of wild flowers; George Borrow, a raconteur of walking travels, most notably *Wild Wales* (1862); Richard Jefferies, whose complicated combination of the realist and the mystic confounds categorisation; George Sturt, who wrote as 'George Bourne', with a dignity that distinguished education about living in the country from 'civilisation' or even 'literacy'; W. H. Hudson, the rambler and naturalist, whose *A Shepherd's Life* (1910) extends observation into subjectivity: '*what we see we feel*'; Edward Thomas, the most complex recorder of alienation who wrote from an awareness of the danger of 'the turning of England into a town with a green backyard' (Keith 1975: 194); Henry Williamson, twenty-one years old when Thomas was killed not a few hundred yards from him at the Battle of Arras, author of *Tarka the Otter* (1927) which went through seventeen revisions 'not for style but for truth'; H. J. Massingham, whose *Shepherd's Country* (1938) constructed what Keith calls 'an ecological foundation of a unified landscape' (Keith 1975: 244).

In his introduction to these writers Keith makes a distinction between their works and the pastoral. His stance is significantly defensive, arguing against idealisation, the case for reality, and against a knowing pastoral stance, for an innocent sincerity that is opposed to 'sophisticated pastoral effects' (Keith 1975: 5). This ignores the context in which these texts were read and the cultural significance they achieved. The cases of Cobbett, Jefferies and Thomas are perhaps an exception, but there can be no doubt that, for the largely urban readers of these representations of English countryside, they acted as a form of pastoral escape from their own urbanised realities. Although Ronald Blythe's *Akenfield* (1969) quotes a villager as saying 'We are all living in the rat-race however far out in the wilds we are', the function of the book is to put urban readers in touch with the experience of those living 'out in the wilds'.

The same must be said of the parallel rural novels of the nineteenth and early twentieth centuries, although there are complex distinctions to be made between and within them. Glen Cavaliero, speaking of the rural novels of the first half of this century, suggests that D. H. Lawrence's *The White Peacock* (1910) and *The Rainbow* (1915) are touchstone achievements which relegate most of the novels he goes on to discuss to those of 'numerous lesser writers'. In fact, because Lawrence's project is nothing less than the reintegration of inner nature with a creative–destructive universe, despite the lyrically pastoral style of the earlier novel, his work can be seen as post-pastoral in its vision. Whilst acknowledging the tradition of Elizabeth Gaskell's *North and South* (1855), George Meredith's *Rhoda Fleming* (1864) and Richard Jefferies's *The Dewy Morn* (1884), Cavaliero might have cited W. H. Hudson's romance of lost nature, *Green Mansions* (1904), as he might have cited the Scottish tradition of rural romance that would include Sir Walter Scott and Lewis Grassic Gibbon. But, again, a quick survey of his novelists indicates the range of forms by which the impulse towards fictional escape has been satisfied at a time when suburbias were creeping across green fields as never before.

The rural fantasies of Kenneth Grahame's *Wind in the Willows* (1908) and T. H. White's *The Sword in the Stone* (1939) present 'delighted accounts of woodland life' that share the sentimentality and whimsy of what Cavaliero calls 'the cult of the primitive' in the Dartmoor novels of Eden Phillpotts and 'John Trevena'. Regionalism was itself an attraction in Hugh Walpole's *Rogue Herries* (1930) novels set in Cumberland and in Sheila Kaye-Smith's Sussex novels begun with *The End of the House of Alard* (1923). The irony that Walpole's popularising of the isolated little settlement of Watendlath above Borrowdale contributed to its being opened up to the motor car is a tension treated by Francis Brett Young in *Undergrowth* (1913) regretting change, and by Winifred Holtby in *South Riding* (1936) where, whilst change is accepted, its motives are questioned. An aspect of change in the countryside of the 1930s was its reflection in a move away from romantic treatments and towards the more georgic writing of farmer novelists such as the three who each published in 1930 a novel about a farm: H. W. Freeman in *Down in the Valley*, A. G. Street in *Farmer's Glory* and Adrian Bell in *Corduroy*.

One benefit of this movement away from sentimentality is the work of two West Country novelists, Henry Williamson and Llewelyn Powys, whose intense personal witness to the power of both observed and felt experience in nature achieves a suggestion of spiritual renewal. Williamson's four 1920s' novels which were collected as *The Flax of Dream* in 1936 are flawed by a pessimism that can become an indulgence in oppression. In Llewelyn Powys, younger brother of John Cooper and T. F. Powys, death is a physical presence that counters the Dorset 'Elysium' of *Love and Death* (1939). The short stories of H. E. Bates represent the continuing popularity of rural fiction, but it was the emotional intensity of the work of T. F. Powys and Mary Webb that drew the satire of Stella Gibbons's *Cold Comfort Farm*. Mary Webb's sub-Lawrencian prose has also remained popular, perhaps because its symbolic force is more accessible, often too accessible. She says of a character in *Gone to Earth* (1917) for example: 'Half out of the soil, minded like the dormouse and the beetle, he was, by virtue of his unspoken passion, the protoplasm of a poet'. The yearning for connectedness with nature is so strong in this overblown style that it hardly needs parody.

The continuing need for a discourse of retreat in the culture is reflected in the choice of pastoral set texts for examination in schools. When the Georgian poets could no longer serve, the popularity of texts such as *Cider with Rosie* performed this function. Laurie Lee's Cotswold village provided a lush and warm environment in which to locate a story of a gentle loss of sexual innocence that is unproblematically characterised by the author as 'wonderful'. Peter Marinelli argued that the popular set text *Lord of the Flies* 'is truly and seriously pastoral in its movement' (Marinelli 1971: 81). He is not applying the term pejoratively, but there is, indeed, something escapist in the fatalism of the novel's suggestion that evil is not a matter of choice. That fascism will result from a retreat into nature by a gang of choir-boys, implies that, since the Serpent will inevitably emerge, even in Arcadia, there is no point in taking Coleridge's difficult and dangerous journey to confront it and to comprehend it with a 'blessing'. The novel demonstrates a fatalistic assumption about a particular class of boys rather than exploring the sources of fascism in ourselves.

The pastoral impulse to escapism as its weakest mode persists in the most surprising forms. R. S. Thomas's retreat into the fields of west Wales in search of God has produced a bleak, reluctant pastoral poetry with which the Welsh literary establishment identifies to the point of idolatry. Parallel to Mackay Brown's hatred of 'Progress' is Thomas's hatred of the capitalised 'Machine'. His preference is for 'turning aside' in the Georgian manner, even as he appears to be resisting a nostalgic pastoral in 'The Bright Field':

> Life is not hurrying
> on to a receding future, nor hankering after
> an imagined past. It is the turning
> aside like Moses to the miracle
> of the lit bush.

Thomas simply imposes 'miracle' upon what Marvell worked hard to evoke in all its ambiguous complexity. Ultimately, R. S. Thomas's poetry, for all his angst in the bleak Welsh fields and hills, is a pastoral escapism from the complexities of relationships with the natural world as much as with the modern world. The simple discourse of 'The Bright Field' is one of imposed religious significance rather than earned insight such as Marvell's.

The case of *The Archers*, as of the *Guardian*'s Country Diary, is worth considering as perhaps sustaining by substituting for the tradition of rural literature in its fiction and non-fiction forms at a time when less than 3 per cent of the population is employed in agriculture. A cultural analysis would reveal that the nature of these two 'texts' does not stay unchanged. The need for 'the townsman' to 'appreciate' the facts and 'diversions' of country life, as the BBC's plan for *The Archers* put it in 1950 (Short 1992: 145), is an expression of the need for a pastoral. But the previously escapist Arcadia of Ambridge now incorporates a debate between the landowner's agribusiness ideology and his daughter's New Age travellers' critique. There is now homophobia in The Bull. The emergence of these changes is perhaps not unconnected with a new generation of writers for the series who are themselves urban incomers to village life. But one might ask why the series persists, and, remembering that an 'Agricultural Adviser' is still necessary, it is hard to avoid the conclusion that *The Archers* still performs for many listeners the function of pastoral retreat as a contemporary georgic. On the other hand, it is interesting to note that the most recent recruits to the *Guardian*'s County Diary are now more scientific than Georgian in their approach to natural history, although its title and the brevity of this little box on the page does still suggest a pastoral function rather than a scientific feature.

In America the possibility of retreat to a rural home outside a commuter village is very much part of the American Dream that combines wealth with social decency and ownership of a parcel of land. Philip Roth's recent novel *American Pastoral* (1997) traces the success of a schoolboy sports hero in taking over the business of his immigrant forefathers and buying a farm 'five hilly miles' outside Old Rimrock village. A model of health, wealth and liberalism, Seymour Levov, the novel's hero, represents the 'anticipated American future' of 'each generation's getting smarter' and 'forming yourself as an ideal person'. His daughter Merry, brought up in the tranquil New Jersey countryside, is raised 'with all the modern ideas of being rational with your children'. Roth presents this as a national utopian ideal to be achieved in retreat from the actual urban location of the factory that is the original source of the family wealth, before a factory in Puerto Rico became an economic advantage. But Roth's novel is an anti-pastoral. Merry Levov becomes involved in the movement against the Vietnam War and 'brings the war home', as the slogan of the time advocated, by blowing up Old Rimrock's village store, killing a man in the blast. The novel is partly an attempt to understand the origins of the radical student violence of 1968 in America that ran parallel to the pastoral 'liberation' of Flower Power, Woodstock and the youth movement of rural alternative living that has developed into some of today's forms of New Age environmental activism. Roth's interest is in Seymour Levov's attempt to understand the failure of the utopian dream of bourgeois retreat that has its American origins in the pastoral literature of early pioneers, travellers and wilderness sages such as John Muir and Henry David Thoreau.

Certain kinds of travel writing and nature writing have been serving a function of pastoral retreat for their readers since their inception. Daniel Defoe's *A Tour Through the Whole Island of Great Britain* (1731) was read with cosmopolitan horror. By contrast, the Native American William Least Heat-Moon's 1982 book about travelling the minor roads of America, *Blue Highways*, was hailed as a 'masterpiece' that his publishers claim 'captures our sense of national destiny'. Henry David Thoreau's retreat in 1845 from urban Concord to Walden Pond 'to front only the essential facts of life, and see if I could not learn what it had to teach', produced *Walden* (1854), the archetypal book of American nature writing and still (in a 1992 survey) the most frequently taught nineteenth-century book on the US curriculum. But a heritage of hermits and pioneers is not essential to the popularity of travel writing. The recent immediate success in the UK of Sara Wheeler's travel book *Terra Incognita* (1996) might be due to her ability to draw explicitly upon what she calls 'the symbolic properties of Antarctica'. She admits that the timelessness of 'a place that knows no degradation', as someone there tells her when they find a mummified young seal, endorses her own explicit sense of Antarctica as Arcadia:

> The absence of decay, such a salient characteristic of my surroundings, reinforced my perception of the continent as a kind of Shangri-La (the residents of which enjoyed eternal youth – also a key element in the legend of the dead Antarctic explorers).

The pastoral nature of this writing is clear from the fact that death is, of course, actually a very real presence in the Antarctic. Wheeler is aware that travel can be 'either a journey of discovery concerned with pushing forward all kinds of boundaries, or an easy-access escape hatch to a primrose path'. It was a treacherously familiar stretch of the psychic landscape. She admits that she does not know what she is looking for, although she calls it 'something more important than myself'. She imagines that it will be found where she is 'loosed from my cultural moorings', yet her book is mostly about the culture that has been 'moored' on the ice by generations of explorers and scientists. The 'higher power' she seeks is a notion she has brought with her, rather than what could be discovered by 'Annihilating all that's made / To a green Thought in a green Shade'.

Similarly, the nature writing of Rick Bass, who writes of the natural life in a valley in Montana where he lives and of his relationship with it, serves a pastoral function for readers whose lives are dependent upon the city even if they no longer need to live there. *The Year of the Yaak* (1995) is his report from his retreat in the tradition of Thoreau and Muir. Like them, Bass has recently been forced to use his pastoral writing in *Fiber* (1998) to defend the location of retreat from external threats. The result is a more complex work that uses an original form to play tricks upon the reader in order to gain their support for a defence of the valley. But the point remains that Bass, like many American nature writers, is completing the cycle implicit in pastoral retreat of a return to the court, the city, the political world. In the best of pastoral literature, the writer will have taken the reader on a journey to be changed and charged upon return for more informed action in the present.

It is possible to regard the work of nature writers as a therapy of retreat. Encouragement to participate in the creative process of writing a 'nature essay' or 'non-fiction story' is offered in *The Sierra Club Nature Writing Handbook* (1995). Information and entertainment is John A. Murray's definition of what is neither quite scholarly nor journalistic nor fictional, although it contains elements of each of these discourses. 'The boundaries of the essay form in contemporary times', Murray says, 'are much broader than they have ever been previously. This is a development to be celebrated, for it shows that literature is growing, just as nature grows.' One might add that this is obviously an expansion in the contemporary discourse of retreat. The question remains as to what insights are brought back by these writers upon their return to their audience. Has the pastoral delivered a delightful escape or a challenge to the conceptions of the urbanised reader?

4

THE CULTURAL CONTEXTS OF RETURN

Whatever the locations and modes of pastoral retreat may be, there must in some sense be a return from that location to a context in which the results of the journey are to be understood. When the pastoral is merely escapist, as in the anthologies of the Georgian poets after the First World War, there is an implicit attempt on the part of the writer to resist return, to stay out there in the safely comforting location of retreat, in their case in the countryside of a mythic Old England where stability and traditional values were located. Because the journey to the country is written for an urban audience, there is intrinsic to the pastoral a movement of retreat and return that, if not explicit within the text, as in the return to court in *As You Like It* and *The Winter's Tale*, is implicit in the address to an audience for whom what happens in Arcadia has some interest. Indeed, whether the author's choice of Arcadia is classical Greece, the only-just-disappeared Golden Age, the present Golden Age, a utopian future, an Alpine summit, Antarctica, Arden or the garden, that choice will be made with its contemporary audience in mind. The discourse of retreat will exploit the location in order to speak to the cultural context of its readership. If the pastoral is successful, the audience will know that what is perceived to be happening in Arcadia has relevance for them in their own time and (urban) place, with its own anxieties and tensions.

This is the essential paradox of the pastoral: that a retreat to a place apparently without the anxieties of the town, or the court, or the present, actually delivers insights into the culture from which it originates. Pastoral authors are inescapably of their own culture and its preoccupations. Thus the pastoral construct always reveals the preoccupations and tensions of its time. Even if it is an unintended reflection, the most determined escape returns something to its audience. The unreality of an Arcadia constructed of 'nothing but joy, and plenty, and contentment' which so disgusted Dr Johnson in 1750, was precisely what Edmund Blunden's generation needed from poetry after the First World War. When in the 1920s Blunden replied, 'And why not?' he was appealing to his audience's fear of the instabilities in English society following that war: weakening class divisions, growing unemployment, women's suffrage, the effects of the car, the countryside in decay, suburban expansion (Blunden 1929: 89). The cultural context in which the pastoral is written provides a way of reading and evaluating the results of pastoral return.

Often associated with the Georgians because his subject was the countryside, because his poetic development coincided with theirs, and because he shared their experience of the trenches, Edward Thomas's poetry never appeared in Marsh's anthologies of *Georgian Poetry* (1912–22). The honesty of Thomas's poetry about a changing rural way of life at the turn of the century distinguishes his sensibility from the Georgians' explicit escapism. Thomas's anxieties, doubts and frank bewilderment complicate a poetry that explores several borderlands: the mythic Old England disturbed by the poet's stark experience of war; a Welsh family background and London birth giving distance rather than identification with the myth of 'England' being supposedly defended; a feeling, like Thomas Hardy's, that faith in continuity had been undercut by modernism's scepticism and delight in the fragmentary; a tension between Hardy's belief in realism and modernism's insistence upon the symbolic in poetry. The result is that Thomas's search for a security in that ancient English countryside produced again and again in the poetry a sense of alienation from what ought to be familiar, a sense of doubt about what he was experiencing, even in the apparent dramatic reality of conversation. In his search for the archetypal figure of the English peasant in 'Lob' he finds an informant who evokes symbolic characters of rural resistance (Robin Hood), pagan spirits (Herne the Hunter), and a historic leader of rural insurrection (Jack Cade), but at the very moment of suggesting that his informant is an incarnation of Lob, he disappears, as the original had done, into an ordinary Wiltshireman. A figure representing pastoral permanence was not available in Thomas's time.

In his study of Edward Thomas, Stan Smith has shown how the ideology of England in the poetry strains between the need for a familiar myth and the uncertainties of class, war and personal identity current in Thomas's society. Often this strain is centred upon the voice of a bird, the stormcock that has displaced the nightingales in 'Bob's Lane', the melancholy reminder of 'soldiers and poor, unable to rejoice' in 'The Owl', and the strange enigma of 'The Unknown Bird'. The latter is a symbol of a landscape which ought to be able to provide stability 'against the ruins', but which appears to be unreal. The bird which sang in the beechwood is disturbing, not only because it cannot be recognised by naturalists, but because Thomas cannot be sure whether its song was sad or joyful: 'But if sad / 'Twas sad only with joy too, too far off / For me to taste it'. The confusion of expression here suggests an unreality in the writer's perception and in his ability to distinguish emotional states. So what should be a comfort becomes instead a temptation to madness:

> This surely I know, that I who listened then,
> Happy sometimes, sometimes suffering
> A heavy body and a heavy heart,
> Now straightway, if I think of it, become
> Light as that bird wandering beyond my shore.

The ambiguity of this ending, with its hint at 'light-headedness', has been anticipated in the bird's song having been described, 'As if a cock crowed past the edge of the world, / As if the bird or I were in a dream'.

So if the retreat of Edward Thomas into the pastoral of the English landscape returns with an image of a world collapsing its supposed certainties to the extent that ephemeral birdsong becomes a key, if unreliable, motif, his poetry has achieved more than that which struggled to keep up the pretence that an unchanged English countryside could provide protection from the starkness of reality. Perhaps the origin of the myth that attracted the Georgians was Shakespeare's English Arcadia, the Forest of Arden in *As You Like It*.

This play begins with unpredictable uncertainties, as three sets of courtiers from three different close relationships are banished from kinship and from court. The Arden they enter is one of economic realities and of open generosity. Corin the shepherd has to explain to the banished Rosalind that his sheepcote is neglected and up for sale and cannot support extra mouths, although he is willing to do what he can to help. The exiled Orlando, on the other hand, meets with an invitation to food that makes an embarrassment of his sword, drawn because 'I thought that all things had been savage here'. Of course, the generosity derives from a court in exile, that of the banished Duke Senior, who makes gracious use of adversity. The song with which this scene ends draws attention to the moral superiority of even a life as harsh as that in the open air of Arden in comparison with the court's inhumanity:

> Blow, blow, thou winter wind,
> Thou art not so unkind
> As man's ingratitude.
> Thy tooth is not so keen,
> Because thou art not seen,
> Although thy breath be rude.
>
> (II. vii. 174)

What we have seen of the court is the intrigue, jealousy and hatred that have led to exile in Arden.

This comparison is set against Touchstone's criteria which provide a satire on the court's preoccupation with manners. The reality of earning a living as a shepherd, Corin must explain, makes the courtly kissing of hands seem absurd: 'They are often tarred over with the surgery of our sheep; and would you have us kiss tar? The courtier's hands are perfumed with civet' (III. ii. 60). Touchstone turns this into a witty courtier's game, as he does the comparison between country and court:

> Truly shepherd, in respect of itself, it is a good life; but in respect that it is a shepherd's life, it is nought. In respect that it is solitary, I like it very well; but in respect that it is private, it is a very vile life. Now in respect it is in the fields, it pleaseth me well; but in respect it is not in the court, it is tedious. As it is a spare life, look you, it fits my humour well; but as there is no more plenty in it, it goes much against my stomach.
>
> (III. ii. 13)

If there is something uneasy about the reasoning of this, it is that court life is valued for its comfort and for itself. Its eloquent structure of contrasts belies the shallowness of court life. Corin is baffled by this rhetoric, but counters with a set of values that are as different as they are simply expressed:

> Sir, I am a true labourer: I earn that I eat, get that I wear; owe no man hate, envy no man's happiness; glad of other men's good, content with my harm; and the greatest of my pride is to see my ewes graze and my lambs suck.
>
> (III. ii. 71)

Shakespeare is using a real pastoral setting as the context for a very different Arden that is, in effect, a court in exile based upon alternative values to that from which Duke Senior, Orlando and Rosalind have been exiled. That these values can heal and transform is evidenced by Orlando's action in the dilemma of saving from the lioness the brother responsible for his exile and Oliver's subsequent transformation, shown in the language with which he describes Orlando's moral choice:

> Twice did he turn back, and purpos'd so.
> But kindness, nobler ever than revenge,
> And nature, stronger than his just occasion,
> Made him give battle to the lioness.
>
> (IV. iii. 127)

Nature in Arden is associated with kindness rather than revenge, which drives the court in its supposedly noble behaviour. Duke Frederick cannot even penetrate Arden. The extremity of his bitterness against his brother Duke Senior requires the extreme antidote of becoming a religious recluse. Arden is the platform from which Jaques can launch his humbling satires on the human condition, which, in their high Renaissance rhetoric, are clearly aimed at both delighting and deflating a court audience.

But the function of Arden in this play is not directly to challenge with an alternative pastoral society, as it is in *The Winter's Tale*. It is to provide a borderland space in which the nature of declarations of love and gender can be tested. In this process each of the distinctive characters finds out who they are and returns to court married not only to their 'true' lovers, but to their better selves. Their distinctiveness is what gives depth to their simple dramatic declarations at the end of the play that together make a voice poem of a diverse, if tangled, society:

> *Silvius*:   And so am I for Phebe.
> *Phebe*:   And so am I for Ganymede.
> *Orlando*:   And so am I for Rosalind.
> *Rosalind*:   And so am I for no woman.
>
> (V. ii. 98)

In Rosalind's ability to untangle these misplaced and inappropriate attachments to each individual's satisfaction she is able to bring harmony to the society of Arden by revealing to each of them their true desires.

Marriage is Shakespeare's dramatic motif for natural harmony, generosity, humility and justice that is taken back into the court. The dance is his dramatic celebration of it. The extent to which an audience feels these qualities have been earned through the process of retreat will determine the extent to which they are convinced these qualities will persist upon the return. Duke Senior's voice, always a slightly suspect one in his tendency to find Johnson's 'nothing but joy' in enduring 'shrewd days and nights' in the forest, can seem glib in his view of the future too:

> Every of this happy number
> That have endur'd shrewd days and nights with us,
> Shall share the good of our returned fortune,
> According to the measure of their states.
> Meantime forget this new-fall'n dignity,
> And fall into our rustic revelry.
> Play music, and you brides and bridegrooms all,
> With measure heap'd in joy, to th' measure fall.
>
> (V. iv. 171)

But one has to remember that Adam nearly died, Orlando saved his brother, and survived, rather successfully, his wooing of a man, Rosalind discovered the male side of her personality, and all emerged apparently intact from Jaques' melancholy satire (which alone could not survive the return and requires a reclusive withdrawal). The final emphasis is on sharing, measured justice, a diversity of 'states', loss of pomposity (which Jaques does not believe possible and is his excuse for slipping away from the return to a new reality), joy and unity. The repeated word 'measure' endorses the notion of balance and harmony which dominates the return.

If the sexual testing at the heart of *As You Like It* makes this pastoral closer to a masquerade, *The Winter's Tale* is a pastoral of a different mode. Here we witness the causes of jealousy growing and infecting the court until none are untouched by it and Leontes has lost his wife, his son, his trusted lord and his baby in a trauma which climaxes at a turning point marked by the famous stage direction 'Exit, pursued by a bear'. On the other side of horror is absurdity and humour. On the other side of this ambiguous dramatic moment are the Shepherd and the Clown who represent the other side of the storm-wracked 'deserts of Bohemia' in which Antigonus leaves the baby Perdita, 'counted lost forever'. Whether this would have been a real bear on loan from the Southwark bear-pit nearby the Globe or not, this moment should have had the effect of producing both surprised momentary terror and a nervous laughter in the audience, so that this turning point is directly experienced with an ambivalence that reflects its symbolic ambiguity. For in Bohemia the storm of negative feedback derived from the court gives way to a natural alternative culture based upon those values first established by Shakespeare in Arden. The difference is that the shepherd community that has adopted Perdita is allowed by the playwright to have the dignity and moral integrity of a fully developed culture that challenges court life. Of course, there are the country clowns that the court audience expects in order ultimately to endorse their own superiority. Indeed, they are essential if the audience is not to feel threatened by a revolutionary impulse in the play's demonstration of a better life outside the court. But Shakespeare has a plot device that will ultimately defuse any threat to his audience from Perdita's central dialogue with Polixenes.

The humanity of the Shepherd's understanding of the behaviour of adolescence in his first speech indicates that we are to be shown more depth in this shepherd community than was allowed in the earlier pastoral. The willingness of this community to accept first the baby Perdita, and later Prince Florizel, leads to Perdita's welcoming to the sheep-shearing feast the stranger who is Florizel's father, Polixenes, in disguise. Perdita's preference for pure breeds of flowers leads to Polixenes defending the process of grafting to 'make conceive a bark of baser kind / by bud of nobler race'. The symbolic irony of this for a father who is resisting his noble son's marriage to a shepherdess will not be lost on the courtiers in the Globe audience. It is in this pastoral community that Polixenes can argue for a grafting of the noble and the base as 'an art that nature makes', a human development of the natural through the human form of creativity that is 'art'. For a moment this revolutionary idea is floated before the audience: that human imagination, and the spirit of natural generosity in this community, could lead to the acceptance of the marriage of a prince to a shepherdess.

But the inner grace that attracted Florizel to Perdita is, of course, not due to her nurture in this society; it is her nature as a princess. Grace, rather than nurture or grafting, becomes the dominant theme of the play and the grace of forgiveness emerges from the humanising movement from the shepherd community back to the court. The possibility of any of the shepherds acquiring the grace of a courtier is safely ridiculed in the characters of Autolycus and the Clown as newly made 'gentlemen born'. The new merchant class at the Jacobean court, who are the product of

Elizabethan capitalism, will not miss the point of this comedy. Nor will those whose political ambition might tempt them to assume the grace intrinsic to royalty as the spectre of civil war grows in the tension between the court and the Commons. In 1614, three years after the first known performance of *The Winter's Tale*, the courtiers had been denounced in the Commons as 'spaniels to the king, and wolves to the people' (Ford 1955: 37). Pastoral's power to satirise social climbers was accompanied by the theatre's use of an ending to idealise the court. However, although there is a necessary closure upon the pastoral alternative in the return to court within the play, the moral momentum of the play towards repentance, forgiveness and respect for inner grace has its origins in the natural largesse, integrity and human possibilities opened up by the process of retreat. The possibilities that might be revealed by a humane 'art' in this process are the subject of *The Tempest*.

Prospero's art is both the cause of his exile on the isle and the means of his own redemption. It is both a power for revenge and a power for reconciliation. It was because he had neglected political realities in his study of esoteric knowledge that Prospero was usurped by his brother Antonio who then sold out Milan to the Duke of Naples. In bringing to the isle not only his own enemies, but Naples's son Ferdinand who immediately falls in love with Miranda, Prospero is manipulating the next generation as a means of healing the enmities in his own. Yet Prospero's isle is so far from Duke Senior's Arden that when Gonzalo attempts a 'sweet are the uses of adversity' speech, imagining himself king of the isle, his friends ridicule what is a self-confessed idealised Golden Age. Gonzalo persists with what is significantly now an outrageous joke at the expense of the pastoral:

> All things in common Nature should produce
> Without sweat or endeavour: treason, felony,
> Sword, pike, knife, gun, or need of any engine,

Would I not have; but Nature should bring forth,
Of its own kind, all foison, all abundance,
To feed my innocent people.

(II. i. 155)

For this island is not only the home of Caliban, the descendant
of Sycorax whose use of education is to learn to curse, but it is a
retreat in which Prospero battles with his rage and the temptation
to revenge. It is Ariel, a spirit who cannot feel, who teaches
Prospero to have pity on the grief being suffered by fathers,
brothers, sons and servants who think each other lost in the storm.
Prospero is shamed into not just compassion, but a self-knowledge
that is to lead to his relinquishing his 'rough magic', his other-
worldliness. Prospero's response is the turning point of this play:

Hast thou, which art but air, a touch, a feeling
Of their afflictions, and shall not myself,
One of their kind, that relish all as sharply
Passion as they, be kindlier mov'd than thou art?
Though with their high wrongs I am struck to th' quick,
Yet with my nobler reason 'gainst my fury
Do I take part: the rarer action is
In virtue than in vengeance: they being penitent,
The sole drift of my purpose doth extend
Not a frown further.

(V. i. 21)

A frowning Prospero has been setting the tone of this retreat,
battling virtue against vengeance in himself, just as Miranda is
paralleled by Caliban, the healing art of music by discordant
natural elements, and the drive to love in Ferdinand by the drive
to ambition in Stephano. When Prospero says of Caliban, 'This
thing of darkness I / Acknowledge mine', he is acknowledging the
darkness in his own frowning nature.

This movement towards self-knowledge in Prospero at the end of the play is triggered by his resolve to break his staff and drown his books, as art gives way to a deeper awareness of nature and the approaching return to the courts of Italy. But the most remarkable dramatic effect, in this magical play of dramatic effects, is the Epilogue in which the play is returned to the audience: Prospero's movement towards humility leaves him exposed on stage pleading with the audience for release from his retreat. He concludes, 'As you from crimes would pardon'd be, / Let your indulgence set me free' (Epilogue). Whether this is an appeal to James I by the writer for indulgence in the matter of having based the plot upon the benign use of magic, or whether it is a reminder to the audience that in reality they are as complicit in the crimes of colonisation they have witnessed as Prospero has been on his isle, the theatrical moment demands of the audience both compassion and guilt. The cultural context of return in *The Tempest* is not indirect as in *As You Like It*, or structural as in *The Winter's Tale*, but direct to the very audience by whose presence it has its life as a drama.

Keats saw this pastoral movement of retreat and return, in which the return from Arcadia delivers insights for the audience that may be surprisingly uncomfortable, but are essentially healing, as the social role of the poet and the function of the poet's art. *Endymion* (1818) is the long pastoral poem with which Keats wanted to seal his reputation, but it is in the unfinished poem 'The Fall of Hyperion' that he explores the difference between the dreamer and the poet. In a dream journey to an ancient, but not a specifically pastoral land, the poet meets the mother of the Muses, Moneta, who points out that his journey has empowered him with the experience of 'What 'tis to die and live again before / Thy fated hour'. The choice for the poet now is either to join the escapists passing their days in 'thoughtless sleep', or to join those to whom 'the miseries of the world / Are misery, and will not let them rest'. This, she elaborates, is the difference between the pastoral dreamer, seeking 'No music but a happy-noted voice', and the poet who must return from his dream to find a useful role as a 'sage, / A humanist, physician to all men'. The poet in the poem feels inadequate to the task, 'as vultures feel / They are no birds when eagles are abroad'. So Moneta challenges him:

> 'Art thou not of the dreamer tribe?
> The poet and the dreamer are distinct,
> Diverse, sheer opposite, antipodes.
> The one pours out a balm upon the World,
> The other vexes it.' Then shouted I
> Spite of myself, and with a Pythia's spleen
> 'Apollo! faded! O far flown Apollo!
> Where is thy misty pestilence to creep
> Into the dwellings, through the door crannies
> Of all mock lyrists, large self-worshipers
> And careless Hectorers in proud bad verse.
> Though I breath death with them it will be life
> To see them sprawl before me into graves'.

This vigorous reversal of the poet's attitude, expressed with devastating verbs and clinching adjectives, is a result of his having accepted his vocation, dangerous and almost overwhelming as it is. Harold E. Toliver is perhaps putting it too much in modern terms when he says that Moneta's message is that 'The poet must come forth from his dreams . . . and speak directly to the social problems of the times: he must put his pastoral vision to use as social therapy' (Loughrey 1984: 128). Certainly 'use' is a concept Keats's poet is aware of when he speaks of the poet's role as 'physician to all men'. But the process Keats is describing in this poem is that of the shamanic journey into the dream world in that scary and wondrous state of trance which Keats knew so well. To fail to return is to remain in a high-flown madness, to have been self-indulgent and to have failed the tribe. Indeed, the whole purpose of negotiating the dream journey is to return, not with social solutions, but with strange stories that mysteriously have the power to heal. For Keats, as for Shakespeare, Blake and Ted Hughes, this is the purpose of art and it describes what happens when the pastoral is working at its most powerful and enigmatic.

Actually, Toliver's terms would apply more accurately to Shelley's desire that his poetry should work as 'social therapy' in both a direct, and at other times indirect, way of 'speaking to the social problems of the times'. When he speaks directly, as in 'The Masque of Anarchy', it is with an explicitly radical politics. His pastoral poetry then becomes an ideal alternative to the abuses of class power and industrial exploitation, just as natural energies in 'Ode to the West Wind' represent potential forces for social change. In 'Epipsychidion' (1821) Shelley creates an Elysian island landscape in which to locate two lovers in an image of natural unity which, he insists, it is possible to recognise as what we call 'reality':

> The Earth and Ocean seem
> To sleep in one another's arms, and dream
> Of waves, flowers, clouds, woods, rocks, and all that we
> Read in their smiles, and call reality.

Here he locates a towered dwelling which is described in terms typical of his hatred of violence:

> 'Tis not a tower of strength, though with its height
> It overtops the woods; but, for delight,
> Some wise and tender Ocean-King, ere crime
> Had been invented, in the world's young prime,
> Reared it.

An awareness of what crime, strength and untenderness can do underpins this passage with obvious implications. Shelley's idealism is intended to be read as pastoral idealisation, but the challenge to the reader is to ask why this cannot become a reality. Indeed, the image of a completely unified, sharing love which he creates becomes an image of universal love so profound as to be beyond articulation. His excitement at his own act of creation overwhelms him at the point where words fail him: 'I pant, I sink, I tremble, I expire!'

Shelley and Keats, the later Romantics, built an allegorical pastoral poetry upon the more direct pioneering example of Wordsworth. In Wordsworth's retreat to Grasmere there was always an intention to mediate to the reader what was to be learned from shepherds about the way the landscape morally educated them. He was even to take the risk of outraging his urban readers, raised on the intricacies of Augustan poetry, by making his style part of his poetic experiment; he would write 'in the language really spoken by men' and the form of the border ballad would be an early model. The final results, in *The Excursion* and *The Prelude*, were so much like didactic narratives of his discoveries that Oscar Wilde remarked that, 'He went to the lakes, but he was never a lake poet. He found in the stones the sermons he had already hidden there.'

Certainly, the flat and abstract verse of *The Excursion* states rather blandly what *The Prelude* famously evokes. The boy in the former learns from a mountain herdsman,

To reverence the volume that displays
The mystery, the life which cannot die;
But in the mountains he did *feel* his faith.
All things, responsive to the writing, there
Breathed immortality, revolving life,
And greatness still revolving; infinite:
There littleness was not; the least of things
Seemed infinite; and there his spirit shaped
Her prospects, nor did he believe, – he *saw*.

The repetition of 'revolving' and 'infinite' actually echoes the verse pattern of the Augustans rather than radically rejecting them.

In the unfinished 'Home at Grasmere' the poet explains that he had no idealisation in mind in making his retreat:

> I came not dreaming of unruffled life,
> Untainted manners; born among the hills,
> Bred also there, I wanted not a scale
> To regulate my hopes; pleased with the good,
> I shrink not from the evil in disgust.

What he actually found among the good is expressed by a typically Wordsworthian balance that owes more to idealistic republicanism than to an anticipation of ecology: 'That they who want, are not too great a weight / For those who can relieve'.

But it is at the climax of 'Home at Grasmere' that Wordsworth struggles to articulate one of the most radical concepts for his pre-Darwinian audience to comprehend. It has been referred to in Chapter 3 in relation to Marvell's 'green Thought in a green Shade', but one has to hear the straining movement of the creative mind excitedly giving birth to this discovery, with all its grammatical contortions, to appreciate what is being delivered from this retreat as the poet is,

> Speaking of nothing more than what we are –
> How exquisitely the individual Mind
> (And the progressive powers perhaps no less
> Of the whole species) to the external world
> Is fitted; and how exquisitely too –
> Theme this but little heard of among men –
> The external world is fitted to the mind;
> And the creation (by no lower name
> Can it be called) which they with blended might
> Accomplish.

For Wordsworth's culture the human mind was what separated us from the animals. Previous images of unity with nature returned by the pastoral were never so radical as this – 'Theme this but little heard of among men'. The idea that our mind is not only a product of nature – indeed, is our 'exquisite' connection with it – but is designed to help us understand our place in nature, is perhaps an explanation of the persistence of the pastoral impulse, in which, as well as the mind, 'the progressive powers . . . of the whole species' are at work. In a sense, the pastoral is that essential 'creation' accomplished with the 'blended might' of both our species' 'progressive powers' and the influence of external nature.

The essential importance of the pastoral in the late eighteenth and early nineteenth centuries might be indicated by the large number of women Romantic poets now being rediscovered. Charlotte Smith's rehabilitation of the sonnet was admired by both Wordsworth and Coleridge. In her work the landscape teaches her to accept her isolation and loneliness as a poet without the mutual support groups available to the male Romantics. The even less well-known Isabella Lickbarrow's *Poetical Effusions* (1814) counted Wordsworth among its subscribers. An inhabitant of Kendal, she retreats in 'A Fragment of Solitude' to find solace for her isolation in exactly the same landscape as Wordsworth, which she celebrates in both its 'secret treasures of earth's fruitful womb' and its 'deep joyless gloom / Of four long dreary months'. In the recently recovered work of these lonely women writers it seems likely that their pastoral poetry returned a sense of solidarity for their female readers similarly cut off from the centres of male social activity.

Seamus Heaney is the successor to Wordsworth, in that he has built upon this idea to develop a poetry that thinks through images of nature as a means to explore love, politics and his role as a writer. Heaney has written two essays on Wordsworth and considered doing post-graduate research on Wordsworth's educational ideas, but his early education had alienated him from his own experience of pastoral County Derry as suitable subject matter for poetry in the latter half of the twentieth century.

> I remember the day I opened Ted Hughes's *Lupercal* in the Belfast University Library. [There was] a poem called 'View of a Pig' and in my childhood we'd killed pigs on the farm, and I'd seen pigs shaved, hung up, and so on . . . Suddenly the matter of contemporary poetry was the material of my own life. I had had some notion that modern poetry was far beyond the likes of me – there was Eliot and so on – so I got this thrill out of trusting my own background, and I started a year later, I think [to write poetry].
>
> (*Ploughshares* 1979, 5, 3: 14)

That Heaney is now a Nobel Laureate and a remarkably popular poet on both sides of the Atlantic is testimony to the continuing need for a pastoral poetry that returns to speak to contemporary concerns. Like Wordsworth, Heaney makes a direct address to his readers with a full awareness of the cultural context in which his work is being read.

In 1972 Heaney gave up full-time university teaching and moved from Belfast to Glanmore in County Wicklow. The accusation of pastoral retreat from the Troubles in the North to the rural South was the stuff of newspaper headlines such as 'Ulster Poet Moves South'. Heaney's eventual reply was in the title of the collection of poems that resulted from the move, *Field Work*. These poems are about living amongst fields rather than the city, but they are both about the work of the domestic enterprise and are themselves the work of a poet finding out for the first time if he could be a full-time writer. That the domestic enterprise echoes that of William and Dorothy Wordsworth's move to Grasmere is recognised and at the same time undercut by Heaney's choosing to quote his wife in 'Sonnet III' of the 'Glanmore Sonnets': 'You're not going to compare us two . . .?' The danger of idealisation is one of the themes of these sonnets and it was explained by Heaney in an introduction to a reading of 'Sonnet III' I recorded at the Cheltenham Literature Festival on 16 October 1982:

> This was the first of the sonnets to be written. I had moved to Wicklow to discover if I could be a full-time writer . . . if I was a writer. All the poems had been coming in a narrow, cramped, tense form on the page. This poem was the first freeing from that. The first two lines came out of the hills and sounded too comfortable, iambic, English even. So I got them at a distance with the next eight lines. I had been to Dove Cottage to do a TV programme and was struck by the similarity of the structure with our cottage in Wicklow. Those last six lines came later.

So the third line is intended to sound a note of warning about the first two:

> This evening the cuckoo and the corncrake
> (So much, too much) consorted at twilight.
> It was all crepuscular and iambic.

But the tension has already been established by the 'too much' which prefaces the tendency to beautify that is latent in the ana-chronistic word 'consorted'. A hint of humour actually prevents 'consorted' from taking itself too seriously as an idealisation: the cuckoo and the corncrake cannot 'consort' in the biological sense. If 'iambic' is intended to hint at the danger of idealising as poetry the voices of birds, it unintentionally does so by being inaccurate. In fact, the call of the cuckoo is a trochee and that of the corncrake is a spondee! Yet there is a sense in which Heaney does feel that there is an organic continuum between the poet's art and natural rhythms experienced at Glanmore.

The discovery of the way language connects with the land is Heaney's mode of responding to the tensions of contemporary

Ireland that have been explicitly confronted in every collection and most famously in *North*. It is the source of continuity that underlies both the marriage poems and the elegies in *Field Work*. An awareness of the danger of idealisation, of finding the iambic where there is none, runs through all the Glanmore sonnets and enables Heaney, after his wife's warning, to conclude 'Sonnet III' with an example of the way natural rhythms can 'refresh' and offer an understanding of the ups and downs of experience in the way that poetry and music can do: 'Outside a rustling and twig-combing breeze / Refreshes and relents. Is cadences.'

Heaney's notion of his art as that of drawing upon the connections that Wordsworth established is characterised in a superb metaphor in the first of the 'Glanmore Sonnets' that are named for the place to which Heaney has committed himself. In his essay 'The Sense of Place' Heaney says of Wordsworth that he 'was perhaps the first man to articulate the nature that becomes available to the feelings through dwelling in one dear perpetual place' (Heaney 1980: 145). 'Sonnet I' works at listening, feeling, tasting, smelling the land to find a 'dream grain' of poetry that is a rhythmic way of working the land (that is, field work):

> Now the good life could be to cross a field
> And art a paradigm of earth new from the lathe
> Of ploughs. My lea is deeply tilled.

The notion of 'paradigm' works two ways here, giving and taking. It is giving expression to the earth itself, whilst taking a pattern for the poem from the earth's rhythms. Sensuous texture, rhythm and poetic form are to be taken from the 'lathe / Of ploughs'. This symbiotic relationship with the earth is present in both the active and passive notions contained in the sentence 'My lea is deeply tilled'. (At a reading in Grasmere in September 1998 Heaney introduced this poem by acknowledging a poem by Osip Mandelstam referring to the poet's voice as a plough, the ultimate pastoral image.) Heaney uses nature imagery not only as subject matter but as his medium for thinking. The process of remaking, mediating through the making of metaphors and sounds in poetry that this poem creates, shows Heaney to be what he claims Wordsworth to be: 'conductor of the palpable energies of earth and sky'. It is these life-sustaining energies that create the warmth and compassion of poems of love and grief that emerge from Heaney's retreat to what his wife calls the 'wilderness' of Glanmore. This is the pastoral source of poems that are to be read in the context of the killings and bigotry of contemporary Ireland that are confronted in *Field Work* by two poems in particular. The first part of 'Triptych' refers to the Nationalist killers of Christopher Ewart-Biggs in July 1976, and 'The Strand at Lough Beg' is written in memory of Colum McCartney, a cousin of Heaney's who was shot dead one night while driving home in County Armagh.

At the end of the latter poem the poet imagines himself kneeling to wash the body with handfuls of dew. Then, 'With rushes that shoot green again, I plait / Green scapulars to wear over your shroud.' Despite the echoing of the lines from Dante's *Purgatorio* which are quoted as the poem's epigraph, the activeness of this grieving, together with the practical use of natural material to hand, save this image from posturing as a classical pastoral scene. But Heaney himself apparently came to doubt this. In the opening sequence of poems in the later book *Station Island*, the ghost of Heaney's cousin appears in order to accuse him of having 'confused evasion and artistic tact',

> for the way you whitewashed ugliness and drew
> the lovely blinds of the *Purgatorio*
> and saccharined my death with morning dew.

This is the most breathtaking accusation of pastoralisation by a poet against himself in modern literature. The poignancy of the poet's guilt, spoken aloud in the voice of his dead cousin, his courage in voicing it, and the implicit attack on his use of nature in *Field Work* as 'evasion' that has 'whitewashed ugliness', are all allowed to stand unchallenged in the later poem. It is a warning, not only from the poet to himself, but to the reader's judgement. As I have said, I found the original a convincing image of practical grief. The potential weakness in Heaney's poetry is one to which a pastoral poet is particularly susceptible, knowing the symbolic value of natural icons so intimately.

There is a danger in *Station Island* that Heaney can ask natural icons to carry too much weight against the 'ugliness' of the political realities. This is when the pantheist, instead of shaping his art from feeling the forces of natural forms, and evoking the evidence for the reader, becomes the nostalgic pastoralist, simply asserting the mysterious, idealised, symbolic power of the old images. In 'Sandstone Keepsake' in *Station Island* a riverbed stone, red with the 'blood' of literary and historical associations, is somehow asked to carry a symbolic weight against the internment camp across the river. Why or how is not at all clear. The result is a vaguely feel-good 'saccharine' against the Troubles.

The best advice the poet gives himself through the voices of the past in *Station Island* is that which finds a natural image for a way forward. The voice of William Carlton interrupts a familiar litany of natural images (alders, mushrooms, dung, 'the melt of shells corrupting') to comment upon this list:

> All this is like a trout kept in a spring
> or maggots sown in wounds –
> another life that cleans our element.

This might stand as a justification for Heaney's form of pastoral poetry at its best. For here is the demand to confront corruption ('the melt of shells', the internment camp, the tank, the interrogator, the killer, that all appear in *Station Island*) through natural images that represent organic processes of dissolution. These images, considered with the discipline of one who knows from Wordsworth that these natural processes are at work in us, can act as a 'cleansing'. The voice of Carlton goes on, 'We are earthworms of the earth, and all that / has gone through us is what will be our trace'. This 'trace' is, of course, what we are left with as a consequence of the pastoral's impulse to return, changed by having processed the culture's corruptions on a retreat into a natural environment at which distance and in which natural context they have begun to be understood.

Thomas Hardy's novels provide interesting examples of the way a 'trace' can reveal more, perhaps, than the writer realises of the tensions of his time, particularly the uncertainty of social position for a product of rural culture like Hardy himself, in the urban culture for which he writes and from which he derives recognition. Actually Hardy had a particularly active part in the rural culture which he mediates for his readers. Hardy followed his father as one of the village fiddlers for the rural ceremonies which he delights in describing for his urban readership. Yet he cannot resist using a character like Grandfer Cantle in *The Return of the Native* (1878) as a kind of comic figure to entertain his readers, at such a pastoral distance that Hardy has to tell his readers to take Grandfer Cantle seriously when he is about to convey some vital plot information, by having the character say, 'I can be an understanding man if you catch me serious, and I am serious now.' The reason for Hardy's patronising attitude towards the shared culture of the natives of Egdon Heath is easy to understand when one realises that in writing *The Return of the Native* he is himself a returned native. He is a self-educated man writing for a literary audience caught in the tension of knowing, but not belonging to, rural culture.

Hardy's local knowledge is evident in the fifth sentence of the novel. Hardy knows the precise moment in the day when, 'looking upwards a furze-cutter would have been inclined to continue work; looking down, he would have decided to finish his faggot and go home.' This opening of the novel impresses the reader with its authenticity. Yet Hardy must also strain to impress the reader with his education by means of a profusion of classical references and some occasional inflated forms of expression. At the end of the second chapter, for example, in trying to suggest the unity of a solitary figure with the skyline on which the figure stands, Hardy produces these two remarkable sentences that distance him from the rural dialect he is about to create vividly for Grandfer Cantle:

> The form was so much like an organic part of the entire motionless structure that to see it move would have impressed the mind as a strange phenomenon. Immobility being the chief characteristic of that whole which the person formed portion of, the discontinuance of immobility in any quarter suggested confusion.

Writing 'the discontinuance of immobility' instead of 'movement' indicates just how uncertain Hardy is that he is at home with the literary London readers of *Belgravia* magazine in which the novel was first serialised.

Of course the matter of position, together with passion and power, provide the major themes of this novel. Confusion and insecurity about social position complicate the passions of the central characters and produce pressures under which crucial decisions are made. The unlikely marriage of Clym, the returned native, and Eustacia, whose desire is to leave the Heath, comes about because both are escaping into abstract ambitions which are fundamentally self-centred. Clym thinks of Eustacia as a partner in the enterprise of starting a school for the village children and she sees him as a way to get to the Paris he has actually repudiated by his returning to Egdon. They are at two stages of the experience of alienation and return. Both are alienated from the Heath and its people whilst both are connected to the Heath by their very nature. Eustacia hates the rural culture, but is completely at home wandering the Heath at night. Clym is alienated because the local people think of him as above them, although he feels nothing but love for the Heath. Clym's ambition is to start a day school for children and a night school for the labourers who, in fact, no longer think of him as 'their kind'. The way Hardy expresses Clym's good intentions renders them suspect from the start:

> Yeobright loved his kind. He had a conviction that the want of most men was knowledge of a sort which brings wisdom rather than affluence. He wished to raise the class at the expense of individuals rather than individuals at the expense of the class. What was more, he was ready at once to be the first unit sacrificed.

The abstract notion of knowledge that will not help these labourers escape their rural poverty, the conviction that does not seek the opinion of the class in question and the self-sacrifice built into the enterprise, all reveal the self-centred and self-destructive nature of Clym's good intentions. In fact, 'the bucolic world', as Hardy rather loftily puts it, has never wanted 'culture before luxury'.

Clym cannot recognise the wisdom to be found in the communal values and sharp perceptions of the class he wishes to raise. Twice local people show themselves to be wiser than Clym. When Clym announces his intentions the Egdonites know that he 'had better mind his business', as one of them puts it. Not being in a listening mode in the role Hardy characterises as 'John the Baptist', Clym ignores Sam's answer to his question as to whether Eustacia would like to teach children: 'Quite a different sort of body from that, I reckon.' But native wisdom is as unemphasised by Hardy as it is ignored by his returned native. As the tragedy of the novel unfolds it is the outcast Diggory Venn who emerges as the hero of the narrative. Clym himself has become an itinerant preacher still seeming to satisfy his own needs rather than those of his listeners.

The remarkable thing about pastoral return in this novel is that the urban audience determined it. The readers of *Belgravia* demanded that, as the final chapter is titled, 'Cheerfulness again assert[s] itself at Blooms-End'. The rather arbitrary implication behind Hardy's phrase 'asserts itself' hints that he finds himself obscuring the point to which the tragic narrative has led by creating a cheerful ending. In the published novel he offered two endings with the suggestion that 'readers can, therefore, choose between the endings and those with an austere artistic code can assume the more consistent conclusion to be the true one.' In the alternative ending Hardy seems to endorse Clym's view that he has been 'ill-used by fortune'. Clym, he says, did not maintain this feeling long, however, because most human beings are reluctant to think that their Creator, or 'First Cause', is a malignant force, 'a power of lower moral quality than their own'. This is an amazing suggestion, but the pessimistic fatalism behind this statement, which has been there all along in those images of people as parasitic insects on the Heath, fails to be ameliorated by the assertion of the healing power of the seasons which is also introduced in the original ending. The fact seems to be that Hardy is himself trapped in the tensions which distort the intense passions and humane values of his central character Clym Yeobright. Inviting his readers to solve his narrative confusion and attributing to a 'First Cause' his own fatalistic hopelessness, is clearly the result of being caught between London and Egdon, between 'literary success' and his native instincts, between the retreat and the return. He is trapped in a bleak borderland, simply not knowing how, under the historical cultural pressures of his time, a man with an awareness wider than his native rural community can make a life for himself which shares those communal values.

At the other end of Britain, a cultural tradition of pastoral verse has been transformed in the late twentieth century to engage with urgent contemporary issues. It should not be ignored here, as it has been by most English critics, simply because it was written in Gaelic. The death in 1996 of the Gaelic poet Sorley MacLean brought to an end a remarkable career in which a pastoral poet was never more aware of the cultural contexts in which his poetry was being read in two languages since the 1930s. The poet and Gaelic scholar Derick Thomson suggests that eighteenth-century Gaelic poets were influenced by the development of English pastoral in the work of Pope and Thomson. Mac Mhaighstir Alasdair (b.1690), who wrote descriptive verse in the form of songs to summer and winter, was following James Thomson's *The Seasons* (Thomson 1977: 157). The praise-song (*Moladh*) for a bard's patron and the patron's lands, which had been strong in the clan system for centuries, was not all that different in function from Pope's 'Windsor Forest'. Inheriting this tradition, Somhairle MacGill-Eain, Sorley MacLean, who was born in 1911 on the island of Raasay, between Skye and the mainland, wrote praise-songs for specific places on Raasay and Skye. His own translations from Gaelic, which some bilingual speakers prefer, indicate that, although he is writing within the cultural frame of reference of Gaelic speakers (the *Gaidhealtachd*) the cultural context of his poetry can be accessible to non-Gaelic speakers with the help of Gaelic scholars. The result is one of the most far-reaching transformations of a pastoral tradition that reflects upon twentieth-century world politics and the nuclear threat in its various forms.

The opening of the long poem 'The Cullin' has its starting point very much within the *Gaidhealtachd*, yet is vivid and moving:

I see the noble island in its storm-showers
As Mairi Mhor saw in her yearning,
And in the breaking of mist from the Garsven's head
Creeping over desolate summits,
There rises before me the plight of my kindred,
The woeful history of the lovely island.

Mairi Mhor, who was known as 'Big Mary of the Songs', was the bard of the land reform movement in the Highlands which was successful in 1885. MacLean was himself born into a family of traditional singers, studied English Literature at Edinburgh University under the influence of an authority on metaphysical poetry and became a Marxist in the 1930s. This is therefore a radical poetry of a symbolist nature which differs from the traditional pastoral praise-song in two respects. Its tone is one of tension derived from personal engagement with what is being praised. This is the beginning of a poem describing a struggle to climb the mountain in which personal struggle with the mountain is transposed to evoke 'the woeful history of the lovely island'. So, secondly, the poem presents the past, not as an idyllic Golden Age for peasant crofters, but as a history of struggle which has a continuity in the present.

The poem was written in 1939 when MacLean conceived the idea for a contemporary Marxist complaint against 'the idea of the conquest of the whole of Europe by Nazi-Fascism without a war in which Britain would not be immediately involved but which would ultimately make Britain a Fascist state'. The fear of the lack of a leadership with a will to go to war against the increasingly successful European fascist movement was at the heart of the poem. So the poet's 'nightmare' which is first referred to in Part II, and in Part VI seems to be the Clearances of the 1850s and 60s, actually becomes the struggle in Spain and beyond. In Part VII the peasants of Minginish are linked to an international vision in which 'the humble of every land / were deceived by ruling-class, State and Civil Law'. Finally the image of the Cullin comes to represent the spirit of potential resistance to the momentum of the historical moment in 1939 when the poet sees a gentle ghost upon the mountain in a tentative and hardly formed image. It is the spirit of a gentle lover, 'the naked ghost of a heart', but it is also 'the ghost of a bare naked brain'. Both love, caring, compassion and rational argument and judgement will be required to face the historical moment of the poem's composition. A celebration of the island's mountain beauty and a personal struggle to climb it has been used to evoke 'a nightmare on the fields' of the island's history of struggle which develops into the present's 'black ooze on the rock face' – MacLean's image for European fascism – before he glimpses a symbolic reminder of human capacities for love and for thought that might enable people to 'rise on the other side of sorrow' as the Cullin seem to do. No pastoral retreat into a celebration of a place could return with a more challenging analysis for its cultural context.

Yet MacLean's achievement is not fully accounted for by this discussion of 'The Cullin'. The range of MacLean's transformation of a pastoral tradition, which is also at the centre of the work of his contemporary Gaelic poets Iain Crichton Smith, Derick Thomson and Donald MacAulay, is facilitated by the way the naming of a place in Gaelic poetry is to evoke a history that is painfully alive today. David Craig's research in *On the Crofters' Trail* (1990) shows how vividly memories of the Clearances are held in oral tradition today by descendants in the Highlands and Gaelic Canada. Even to refer to a birch tree in the opening stanza of a poem titled 'Hallaig' is to touch upon a density of historical feeling and a wide potential of symbolic implication:

> The window is nailed and boarded
> through which I saw the West
> and my love is at the Burn of Hallaig,
> a birch tree, and she has always been.

This poem touches a raw nerve to a Gaelic speaker. The Gaelic scholar John MacInnes explains that 'between 1852 and 1854 the entire population of twelve townships, ninety-four families in all, were driven from their homes' on Raasay (*Calcagus* 2: 32). Hallaig was one of those townships, cleared like the others, by George Rainy, the Highland son of a minister father, who also planted the

pine trees in the south-west of the island. The birch tree comes to
represent in the poem, firstly, 'my love' a potentially healing force
that will come as 'a vehement bullet' at the end of the poem;
secondly, a continuity of island girls in general, 'their laughter a
mist in my ears'; thirdly, the birch wand that traditionally links the
living with the dead in the ballads; fourthly, the indigenous woods
as opposed to the species introduced for profit by an exploitative
landowner; fifthly, the indigenous culture which was wiped out in
two years by the minister's son, the 'great pietist of Screapadal'.
The final irony for the student of pastoral is that this brutal and
widespread clearance of people was perpetrated in order to stock
the land with sheep.

But it is in the poem 'Screapadal' that MacLean makes his most
radical extension of what might be done within the pastoral form
of the Gaelic praise-song. 'Screapadal' takes the nineteenth-century
politics of 'Hallaig' into the twentieth century of Hiroshima. If
'Hallaig' is a poem of outrage and affirmation, 'Screapadal' is a
warning that the social forces that produced the Clearances could
produce the ultimate clearance – *an leirsgrios* – the holocaust of
nuclear war.

> Rainy left Screapadal without people,
> with no houses or cattle, only sheep,
> but he left Screapadal beautiful;
> in his time he could do nothing else.

The 'greed and social pride' that has been attributed to Rainy's
generation is, the poet suggests, still alive and could determine the
use of the nuclear submarines from Faslane naval base which use
the Sound of Raasay for testing in the deepest sea-channel in the
Hebrides. The way this idea is introduced in the poem shows how
MacLean can move from pastoral images, to a stark present, to a
threatened future, and back to the historical threat of which this
is a latest incarnation:

A seal would lift its head
and a basking-shark its sail,
but today in the sea-sound
a submarine lifts its turret
and its black sleek back
threatening the thing that would make
dross of wood, of meadows and of rocks
that would leave Screapadal without beauty
just as it was left without people.

John MacInnes says that MacLean never produced a neologism in Gaelic, but that he has 'invented his own diction' and 'there are times when he appears to be pushing Gaelic to its limits' (Ross and Hendry 1986: 145). In this poem the traditional Gaelic pastoral form is engaging with new dangers. There is a sense that innovation in language and adaptation of form are needed to confront new threats to the very descendants of people and place that were the subject of Gaelic praise-songs of the past. Here, then, is a contemporary pastoral poetry from the north-west Highlands written in a minority language that is equal to some of the most crucial cultural problems of our time, including the ultimate threat to pastoral, the long-term desecration of Arcadia and the inability to return to a recognisable human society.

Finally, one might ask if the quality of meditation that arose from Sorley MacLean's climb on his native Cullin hills is to be found in the sub-genre of travel writing that is mountaineering literature. Certainly the sport has attracted from its beginnings literary figures who have contributed to its literature from Leslie Stephen (*The Playground of Europe*, 1871), through I. A. Richards (*Goodbye to Earth*, 1958) to A. Alvarez (*Feeding the Rat*, 1988) and David Craig (*Native Stones*, 1987). What distinguishes this literature from escapist, entertaining travel writing about hiking such as Bill Bryson's *A Walk in the Woods* (1997), is a slightly higher risk of death than even Bryson can imagine. The original impulse, however, might be much the same: 'Why do we go to the hills? To get away from a world which is changing too fast to deliver a sense of continuity. It is no accident that as the world becomes increasingly manic more and more people find the hills a comfort.' This is Phil Bartlett, in his wide-ranging study of this question, *The Undiscovered Country* (1993), providing one obvious answer that would define mountaineering literature as pastoral were there not a certain uncomfortable adversity also involved, not to mention the possibility of the trauma of a personal struggle to survive. The result of the combination of concentration on technical upward movement and the sudden apprehension of beauty, or of the nearness of death, enables a return from the journey with, amongst other possible insights, either an almost religious altered awareness, or an existential sense of at-homeness, or an enlargement of the psychic landscape, or the discovery of other capacities in the self's engagement with the mountain environment that enables survival against the odds.

W. H. Murray's *Mountaineering in Scotland* (1947) was written in a wartime prison camp where he recalled, among other ascents, a night climb on Buachaille Etive Mor above Rannoch Moor when at the summit the mist sunk below him and 'the clear moon burst from a clear sky':

> Something in that night cried out to us, not low, nor faltering, but clear, true, urgent – that this was not all: that not half the wonder had pierced the clouds of our blindness; that the world was full of a divine splendour, which must be sought within oneself before it might be found without: that our task was to see and know. From the deeps of the earth to the uttermost star above the whole creation had throbbed with a full and new life . . .

This chapter is titled 'The Evidence of Things Not Seen' and this experience is presented by Murray as evidence of his own inadequacy: 'Something underlying the world as we saw it had been withheld. The very skies had trembled with presentiment of the last reality; and we had not been worthy.' David Craig quite rightly points out that there is no 'last reality' (Craig 1987: 140); this was all there is, sufficient unto itself in its existential beauty. Murray had not been 'unworthy' in some way – quite the opposite, as his articulation of the experience shows.

David Craig himself has caught the experience of existential at-homeness that the body's close reading of a rockface or a mountain form can lead to:

> When I sit on a six-inch ledge with my feet dangling above a two hundred foot drop, the hart's-tongue fern and dwarf hawthorn a few inches from my eyes, the air smelling of moss, wood-pigeons clattering out of the tree-tops down below, then at least for a time I have grafted myself back into nature, and the sense of rightness achieved, or regained, is unmistakable.
>
> (Craig 1987: 6)

The word 'achieved' indicates that this experience is the result of the exercise of a certain discipline that combines craft and alertness with physical effort and mental control. The great writer about the latter struggle between effort and fear was the psychologist Menlove Edwards whose essays of self-exploration modestly appeared in his club journal, but have been anthologised for a wider audience. He returned from a retreat to make a new climb alone in the mountains of North Wales to his Liverpool home with a startling capacity for expressing not just the schizophrenia of boldness and caution that is balanced by the climber, but the insights that can result. After giving way to caution on a new climb, he concludes 'A Great Effort' with this positive resolve:

> But the resilience of man is great, and his ingenuity. So I was not done yet and on the way back settling to work I soon picked

> up my pride in this way, by thinking, today the victory has been
> to the devil, but tomorrow is not to him yet, also by thinking,
> it has been said that the secret of life is in detachment from it,
> good.
>
> (Gifford 1997: 283)

This idiosyncratic style has been deployed to describe the mental and emotional struggle of standing in one place for an hour and a half, unable to move up, that has been the subject of most of the essay. This is perhaps unlikely pastoral. But more so must be the books that chart a fight for life over several days that can gain huge popularity with a wide readership such as Joe Simpson's *Touching the Void* (1988). The Romantic tradition of mountaineering writing, of which Murray's work is obviously a part, was, from the beginning, qualified occasionally by both a dry, scientific prose and a British taste for understatement, the latter culminating in H. W. Tilman's 1937 summit statement: 'I believe we so far forgot ourselves as to shake hands on it.' Joe Simpson's mixed emotions on a summit in the Peruvian Andes catch the way the turning point of a mountaineering journey is usually a return to begin another journey towards pleasure and fear:

> We took the customary photos and ate some chocolate. I felt
> the usual anticlimax. What now? It was a vicious circle. If you
> succeed with one dream, you come back to square one and it's
> not long before you're conjuring up another, slightly harder,
> a bit more ambitious – bit more dangerous. I didn't like the
> thought of where it might be leading me. As if, in some strange
> way, the very nature of the game was controlling me, taking me
> towards a logical but frightening conclusion; it always unsettled
> me, this moment of reaching the summit, this sudden stillness
> and quiet after the storm, which gave me time to wonder at
> what I was doing and sense a niggling doubt that perhaps I
> was inexorably losing control – was I here purely for pleasure

or was it egotism? Did I really want to come back for more? But these moments were also good times, and I knew that the feelings would pass. Then I could excuse them as morbid pessimistic fears that had no sound basis.

When the writer returns to explore the trap of the pastoral impulse in the mountaineer, he is perhaps expressing in an extreme form the need – and anxiety about that need – in every ordinary walker or rambler who has ever got lost, been overwhelmed by bad weather, or had a glimpse of Arcadia's capacity to turn into Hell.

Simpson did not need to fear future journeys to experience the doubts about losing control. In descent he broke a leg, was lowered over a crevasse by his partner who had no realistic choice but to cut the rope and, passing, the following day, the crevasse into which he had dropped Simpson, give him up for dead. *Touching the Void* is a first book, written upon return in a dramatic form using the two voices of the climbers and in a vividly economical style, that charts the discovery of inner resources that enabled Simpson to crawl into base camp just as it was being evacuated. The function of this hugely popular book, for readers who are, in the main, not mountaineers, is clearly the revelation of unknown personal qualities from a retreat to a beautiful but dangerous Arcadia. The vicarious catharsis derived from mountaineering 'escapist' writing can be that of Greek tragedy. With pastoral books as austere as Simpson's, who needs anti-pastoral literature?

5

THE ANTI-PASTORAL TRADITION

The Victorian poet Matthew Arnold, in his long poem 'Thyrsis' (1867), mourns the death of his poet friend Arthur Clough by describing how, in their youth together, they roamed the fields outside Oxford in the roles of Sicilian shepherds, playing on Dorian pipes and amazing the local farm labourers who may not have realised that they were working in an Oxfordshire Arcadia:

> Too rare, too rare, grow now my visits here,
>   But once I knew each field, each flower, each stick;
>   And with the country-folk acquaintance made
>   By barn in threshing-time, by new-built rick.
>   Here, too, our shepherd-pipes we first assay'd.
>   Ah me! this many a year
>   My pipe is lost, my shepherd's holiday!
>   Needs must I lose them, needs with a heavy heart
>   Into the world of men and waves of men depart;
>   But Thyrsis of his own will went away.

Of course, Clough was Thyrsis – 'for Corydon no rival now!' – and in the manner of a pastoralisation he simply 'of his own will went away' (Clough did not commit suicide).

This reference back to the earliest pastoral of Theocritus, whose Sicilian shepherd Corydon we met in the opening of Chapter 2, is also a reminder that these scholars were re-enacting the 'shepherd's holidays' of Elizabethan pastorals with an awareness that there must come a return to the 'world of men and waves of men' in the city. This pastoral of youth, with its detail of Oxfordshire flora and place nostalgically constructing this Arcadia, keeps the tone of mourning at a softer distance from the disillusioned anguish of Tennyson's 'In Memoriam'. 'Dover Beach' is Arnold's famous poem about the weakening of his religious faith by the author of *Culture and Anarchy* (1869) who believed that human high culture, such as religious art, for example, kept the species from its potential animal anarchy. However, in the light of Arnold's faith in an Arcadian nature to buttress him against grief, 'Dover Beach' (written 1851) is as much a loss of faith in nature as the source of cultural value as it came to be for Sorley MacLean and Seamus Heaney.

The poem begins by constructing a vision of nature that has a positive effect upon the speaker to the extent that he wants to share it with his lover. Indeed, the poetry is exemplary in using technique to create the rhythms and sounds of the sea. But what begins as calming, even 'tranquil', turns into a 'grating roar' that brings to the speaker a sadness at, presumably, the 'eternal' repetition of natural violence:

> The sea is calm to-night.
> The tide is full, the moon lies fair
> Upon the straits; – on the French coast the light
> Gleams and is gone; the cliffs of England stand,
> Glimmering and vast, out in the tranquil bay.
> Come to the window, sweet is the night-air!

> Only, from the long line of spray
> Where the sea meets the moon-blanch'd land,
> Listen! you hear the grating roar
> Of pebbles which the waves draw back, and fling,
> At their return, up the high strand,
> Begin, and cease, and then again begin,
> With tremulous cadence slow, and bring
> The eternal note of sadness in.

The word 'Only' seems to be acting as 'Only spoiling this tranquillity' created by sea, moon, cliffs, and night-air in harmony. It is where the sea meets the land that violence takes place and by the end of the poem this will have come to represent the whole natural world as a battleground of neutral forces in continuous conflict.

The classical reference Arnold now introduces is not a comforting pastoral one, but the suggestion that when Sophocles heard this sound, 'it brought / Into his mind the turbid ebb and flow / Of human misery'. Arnold recognises that this is imposing on the sound 'a thought', but goes on to develop his own version of that thought, appropriate to 'this distant northern sea', just as a pastoralist might have done in the role of his classical predecessor examining a current social anxiety. Arnold's concern seems to be both personal and social, a result, perhaps, of a general decline in religious belief at the end of the nineteenth century in the face of Darwinian science, philosophical rationalism, and a disturbing sense of rapid social change:

> The Sea of Faith
> Was once, too, at the full, and round earth's shore
> Lay like the folds of a bright girdle furl'd.
> But now I only hear
> Its melancholy, long, withdrawing roar,
> Retreating, to the breath

> Of the night-wind, down the vast edges drear
> And naked shingles of the world.

Girdling the whole earth was a belief that God was good, indeed, that God had made the earth within a benign creation, and this faith, shared by most of the 'cultured' world in Arnold's terms, seemed to hold the culture's construction of the natural world together. The retreat of faith leaves Arnold, not with a religious image of a comfortable 'shore' full of promise and hope, but with 'vast edges drear' as though he has looked over the edge of the world to see only 'naked shingles' where nothing lives or grows or could have joyous life. This is effectively the breaking of the possibility of the pastoral. It leaves Arnold clinging only to a belief in the commitment of human love with the desperation of what amounts to a plea:

> Ah, love, let us be true
> To one another! for the world, which seems
> To lie before us like a land of dreams,
> So various, so beautiful, so new,
> Hath really neither joy, nor love, nor light,
> Nor certitude, nor peace, nor help for pain;
> And we are here as on a darkling plain
> Swept with confused alarms of struggle and flight,
> Where ignorant armies clash by night.

'Ignorant' is the key to understanding the depth of Arnold's horror at his discovery of the neutrality of a nature that cannot be invested with that long list of pastoral comforts. To describe the forces of nature as 'ignorant' is to admit that they do not possess an intrinsic drive towards the harmony of a heavenly plan. It is as though we are a species swept along in a struggle for survival together with the ignorant armies of apes from which we derive. The twilight plains of 'ignorant' Africa are perhaps the source of the image in Arnold's mind.

To the extent that Arnold has produced a poem that is ultimately a corrective to his earlier pastoral view of nature, 'Dover Beach' is an anti-pastoral poem. That the natural world can no longer be constructed as 'a land of dreams', but is in fact a bleak battle for survival without divine purpose, is a position which places Matthew Arnold in a tradition of anti-pastoral poets which includes Goldsmith and Crabbe in the eighteenth century, runs from John Clare to Patrick Kavanagh in the twentieth century, and from Blake to Ted Hughes in contemporary poetry. In the USA a tradition of anti-pastoral constructions of the West would include the contemporary novels of Cormac McCarthy and the nature writing of Edward Abbey. Within the tradition there is a strain of satires of the pastoral that runs from Sir Walter Ralegh through Byron to Stella Gibbons's novel *Cold Comfort Farm* and individual poems such as Wendy Cope's 'Pastoral' ('I wish I was a provincial poet / Writing a lot about nature') and Simon Armitage's 'Why write of the Sun' ('when all it has done for us this last year / is dawdle in rain water smeared on the windscreen'). Not to be confused with anti-pastoral are texts that might be characterised as the opposite of pastoral in that they entail a journey to a kind of underworld and return harrowed rather than renewed. Apart from the classical examples of Odysseus and Orpheus, Lear's experience on the 'Blasted Heath' would be an example of an opposite momentum to pastoral that was not intended to be an anti-pastoral corrective in a dialectical relationship with the pastoral. These texts are therefore outside the scope of this book since they make no engagement with the pastoral convention.

Apart from passages of realistic anti-pastoral within classical pastorals (such as Theocritus's reminder that 'Wherever you tread the ground's one thorny ambush' in his Sicilian Arcadia) the first major work of anti-pastoral was written by the Wiltshire farm labourer Stephen Duck. The purpose of *The Thresher's Labour* in 1736 was to give a worker's reply to the eighteenth-century idealisation of the reaper. Duck repudiates the idealisation of the English countryside:

No Fountains murmur here, no Lambkins play,
No Linnets warble, and no Fields look gay;
'Tis all a gloomy, melancholy Scene,
Fit only to provoke the Muse's Spleen.

Pope, it will be remembered, told his urban audience that 'Ceres'
gifts in waving prospect stand, / And nodding tempt the joyful
reaper's hand'. James Thomson, in *The Seasons* (1727), had
described the corn harvest as an erotic event of 'happy Labour,
Love, and social Glee' in which 'the ruddy Maid, / Half naked
swelling on the Sight' stands by her reaper lover, ready to rake up
the results of his 'happy Labour'. Duck uses the Augustan form,
including plenty of classical references, in order to gain acceptance
as a self-taught answer to Pope and Thomson. But, more to the
point, he manages to introduce streams of sweat into Augustan
poetry as his version of Pope's 'joyful reaper' turns to the threshing:

Now in the Air our knotty Weapons fly,
And now with equal Force descend from high;
Down one, up one, so well they keep the Time,
The Cyclops' Hammers could not truer chime;
Nor with more heavy Strokes could Ætna groan,
When Vulcan forg'd the Arms for Thetis' Son.
In briny Streams our Sweat descends apace,
Drops from our Locks, or trickles down our Face.

Duck wrote this poem after days of work actually threshing. But
Duck's final fate was to be taken up by Queen Caroline and
installed in a thatch-roofed pavilion in the Royal gardens as a guide
who peddled pastoral lines such as, 'No plund'ring Armies rob
our fruitful Plain; / But, bless'd with Peace and Plenty, smiles the
Swain'. The 'we' of the vigorous verse above eventually became
transformed into 'the Swain' of the literary convention. But Duck,
in turn, had a rejoinder from Mary Collier in *The Woman's Labour:
An Epistle To Mr Stephen Duck* (1739). Duck had written that after

a day's haymaking 'Next Day the Cocks appear in equal Rows'. Mary Collier replied that it was the women who made them suddenly appear next day. After a brief mid-day break,

> soon we must get up again,
> And nimbly turn our Hay upon the Plain;
> Nay, rake and prow it in, the Case is clear;
> Or how should Cocks in equal Rows appear?

Donna Landry argues that labouring-class women poets such as Mary Collier, a laundress, and Ann Yearsley, a milkwoman, transformed the georgic, not just in producing 'a counter-discourse to this class-conscious, largely masculine tradition', but in helping 'produce transformations within the georgic mode' (Landry 1990: 23). 'What is distinctive about female plebeian georgic is its protofeminist insistence upon the injustice and absurdity of sexual relations as they cut across and adumbrate oppressive class relations' (Landry 1990: 28). The role of the writing of anti-pastoral verse for these female poets is as much a defiance of its male form as it is to satisfy their desire for class or georgic realism.

Goldsmith's long poem *The Deserted Village* (1770) suffered, in effect, a similar fate to that of Duck's poem in the response from Mary Collier. Written as an anti-pastoral it came to be read as a pastoral. Discussed at the end of Chapter 2 as an example of an Arcadia, Goldsmith's imaginary, but representative village, Auburn, had been cleared of its inhabitants by enclosure. But before he idealised the villagers and village life as a repository of communal values, Goldsmith's anti-pastoral intention was carried with some force by a poetry of protest against inhumane agricultural change that altered the land itself:

> One only master grasps the whole domain,
> And half a tillage stints thy smiling plain;
> No more thy glassy brook reflects the day,
> But choked with sedges, works its weedy way.

The 'stinting' of the plain and the 'choking' of the brook represent concrete images for economic effects on the land that also suggest a change in feeling which will be developed in human detail later in the poem.

Raymond Williams was unconvinced by these images:

> But the actual history, in which the destruction of the old social relations was accompanied by an increased use and fertility of the land, is overridden by the imaginative process in which, when the pastoral order is destroyed, creation is 'stinted', the brook is 'choked', the cry of the bittern is 'hollow', the lapwing's cries 'unvaried'. This creation of a 'desert' landscape is an imaginative rather than a social process; it is what the new order does to the poet, not to the land.
>
> (Williams 1975: 100)

There are two points that might be made in reply to Williams. Goldsmith is not claiming that 'creation' is stinted, but that monoculture has stinted the diversity of previous land use by more than one master. In fact, John Clare also uses the word 'desert', twice in the poem 'Remembrances', to describe the change that enclosure had brought to the land and its people. There is no reason, therefore, to disbelieve the contemporary detail that the plough had reduced grassy hillocks to a 'desert' of levelled monoculture. The important point is that we are dealing here with an artistic expression of social history. Goldsmith is offering images of a moment in history, not just for their historical documentation, but because these images evoke the very feeling of that experience for those it affected directly. Thus 'desert' also signifies 'unpeopled'. This represents what people have done to people in a landscape pastoralised by others. Goldsmith's poetry urgently, though often melodramatically, seeks to convey the bitterness of those dispossessed by enclosure. Clouded as this might be by the poem's pastoral structure of retreat and regret, and by his idealisation of village characters, his purpose was to create a political anti-pastoral.

Goldsmith's sharp political use of the Augustan couplet exposed the callousness behind the new commercial approach to agriculture:

> But times are alter'd; trade's unfeeling train
> Usurp the land and dispossess the swain;
> Along the lawn, where scatter'd hamlets rose,
> Unwieldy wealth and cumbrous pomp repose;
> And every want to opulence allied,
> And every pang that folly pays to pride.

What Goldsmith is punching home here rather heavily with his alliteration and rhyming opposites ('unfeeling train' / 'swain'; 'hamlets rose' / 'pomp repose') is the supplanting of village values by the culture of exploitation. An ideology based upon people has been replaced by one based upon efficient use of the land. The new attitude to the land is summed up by Goldsmith in a couplet which, changing metaphor into metonymy, assumes the fate of the land includes the fate of its workers:

> Ill fares the land, to hast'ning ills a prey,
> Where wealth accumulates, and men decay.

The starkness of 'men decay' has the metonymic effect of regarding men as natural plants which are uncared for and 'when once destroy'd, can never be supplied'. Goldsmith's notion of nature is also a notion of humanity that fires his outrage. In his view, wealth derived from such an uncaring attitude to nature will inevitably lead to 'pomp', 'opulence' and 'pride'.

It was Goldsmith's going on to describe what had been lost in nostalgic, idealised and unproblematic terms that led George Crabbe to attack *The Deserted Village* in his own poem *The Village*

(1783). When Goldsmith wrote that for the man working before enclosure, 'For him light labour spread her wholesome store, / Just gave what life requir'd, but gave no more', Crabbe felt that he did not know what he was writing about. Crabbe had read Duck and knew that 'light labour' hardly matched the evidence of 'Streams of Sweat' from the labourer himself. Thirteen years after *The Deserted Village*, Crabbe published *The Village* as a direct anti-pastoral reply to Goldsmith:

> Yes, thus the Muses sing of happy swains,
> Because the Muses never knew their pains:
> They boast their peasants' pipes; but peasants now
> Resign their pipes and plod behind the plough;
> And few, amid the rural-tribe, have time
> To number syllables, and play with rhyme;
> Save honest DUCK, what son of verse could share
> The poet's rapture and the peasant's care?

The contrast in this last line indicates that Crabbe is going to distort in the opposite direction, denying that there is any music at all in his village, that only the rural worker himself can have any credibility in writing about the country, and that the only choice is between 'the poet's rapture and the peasant's care': 'Can poets soothe you, when you pine for bread, / By winding myrtles round your ruin'd shed?' The myrtle, which barely grows in England and is associated with the Mediterranean settings of the classical pastoral, is Crabbe's bathetic indicator of not just the irrelevance of the pastoral to rural poverty, but the cruelty of its intervention between 'pine for bread' and 'ruin'd shed'. 'Winding myrtles' in the construction of an Arcadia out of rural poverty is an activity of crass inhumanity, according to Crabbe. His claim is, 'I paint the Cot, / As Truth will paint it, and as Bards will not.' The assumption is that he is not himself a 'Bard' when he goes on to evoke rural depression in the fashionable images of tolling bells and moping owls for the melancholy taste of his late eighteenth-century readers.

Crabbe was domestic chaplain to the enclosing landowner of villages around Belvoir Castle in Leicestershire, the Duke of Rutland. In the second book of *The Village* Crabbe makes reference to the death of a relative of his patron and goes on to preach to the very people he had been so vigorously defending in the first book:

> And you, ye poor, who still lament your fate,
> Forbear to envy those you call the great;
> And know, amid the blessings they possess,
> They are, like you, the victims of distress.

It is clear that Crabbe's defence of the poor is not only compromised by his own need to write like this on occasions, but that he cannot, in his position, focus upon the causes of rural poverty as Goldsmith had done. Indeed, one must remember that Crabbe's target in the opening of *The Village* was never the consequences of economic change. His strength was the quality of his attack on an idealising literary tradition:

> No shepherds now, in smooth alternate verse,
> Their country's beauty or their nymphs' rehearse;
> Yet still for these we frame the tender strain,
> Still in our lays fond Corydons complain,
> And shepherds' boys their amorous pains reveal,
> The only pains, alas! they never feel.

But against this, Crabbe's original impulse towards an indignant and caring intention to at least paint 'the real Picture of the Poor' gives way to preaching the same acceptance of the status quo that had been the function of the seventeenth-century pastorals of the great houses. Clearly the anti-pastoral tradition at its height displays a tension that will recur to the present: it is caught between notions of realism and poetic conventions, between authenticity of voice and the temptation to become 'Bard', and ultimately between attack and analysis.

John Clare would appear to be in a position to outflank these traps in his idiosyncratic poetry that creates its own conventions and speaks from the experience of a Northamptonshire farm labourer and from the detail of his intimate knowledge of his parish, Helpston. Yet the pressure was put upon Clare to, in Charles Lamb's advice, 'transplant Arcadia to Helpstone. The true rustic style, the Arcadian English, I think is to be found in Shenstone.' Shenstone was an eighteenth-century estate-owner who wrote pastoral verse endorsing the possession of nature by the workers in it:

> The fragrance of the bean's perfume,
> Be theirs alone who cultivate the soil,
> And drink the cup of thirst, and eat the bread of toil.

In fact, Clare wrote a poem titled 'Pastoral Poesy' in order to find 'a language that is ever green' to set against the temptation to idealise the countryside of his childhood that had been lost to enclosures:

> Fancy spreads Edens whereso're they be;
> The world breaks on them like an opening flower,
> Green joys and cloudless skies are all they see;
> The hour of childhood is the rose's hour.

The self-awareness of this is what is fed into Clare's refusal to pastoralise the bitter experience of agricultural and social change. In 'The Mores' Clare's clear eye and alert mind show how it feels to suffer 'the rage of the blundering plough':

Now this sweet vision of my boyish hours
Free as spring clouds and wild as summer flowers
Is faded all – a hope that blossomed free
And hath been once no more shall ever be
Inclosure came and trampled on the grave
Of labourers rights and left the poor a slave
And memorys pride ere want to wealth did bow
Is both the shadow and the substance now.

The loss is not just of boyhood innocence, but of hope, rights and freedom to subsistence grazing on 'the moors' that were the commons. The effects are deeply social: 'And every village owns its tyrants now, / And parish-slaves must live as parish kings allow.' Clare's poetry records an alienation from a countryside now drained, cleared of trees, meadows and rights of way and signified by fences, 'no road here' signs, straightened streams, and bald acres under plough. That personal alienation was brought almost to breaking point by Clare's being taken up by London society as a pastoral 'peasant poet', then ridiculed and finally neglected in his decline in the asylum.

Thus far the anti-pastoral tradition might appear to be based simply upon exposing the distance between reality and the pastoral convention when that distance is so conspicuous as to undermine the ability of the convention to be accepted as such. But that distance can be caused, not only by economic or social realities, but by cultural uses of the pastoral that an anti-pastoral text might expose. An example of an anti-pastoral text that bitterly attacks a form of cultural pastoral that leads to emotional alienation was written by an Irish farmer who has been one of the influences in the work of Seamus Heaney. Alienation from the familiar and loved land is the theme of the Irish poet Patrick Kavanagh in his 1942 poem *The Great Hunger*. The title refers not to the potato famine of the 1840s but to the emotional and sexual hunger of a County Monaghan potato farmer of the 1930s. Guilt and fear of his sexual nature alienate Patrick Maguire from the teeming nature that he works amongst. His mother mediates the Catholic Church's notion of his existence as being in some kind of harmony with nature in an innocence before the Fall when she encourages him to think of himself as 'a man who made the fields his bride'. In fact, 'the grip of irregular fields' has made his flesh clay, as the opening line of the fourteen-part poem suggests: 'Clay is the word and clay is the flesh'. But this apocalyptic line, balancing the abstract 'word' against the material 'flesh', is immediately at odds with the deflation of the potato-gatherers as 'mechanised scare-crows' that follows. The biblical is undercut by the anti-Romantic language in a way that seems to work through the linking notion of 'clay' and its literal down-to-earthness. This shift in tone is typical of the way different parts of the poem adopt different registers and modes of address, with varying degrees of success.

At the centre of *The Great Hunger* is an attack on the way the Church has pastoralised nature as part of the process of taking over an innate pantheism and repressing sexuality. Maguire's mother mediates the Church's teaching by telling her son that confession copes with sexuality. 'And all the while she was setting up the lie / She trusted in nature that never deceives.' The despair and frustration of Maguire's 'broken-backed' life in his fields is all the more poignant because he does experience glimpses of a natural connection with his land in visionary moments when, Kavanagh admits, 'These men know God the Father in a Tree'. But this is not the potentially enlarging pantheism it might seem since the language indicates the overlaying of a naturally special moment with Catholic symbolism. Its corollary notion is 'sin', with its consequent practical double standards in those who have learned that 'Religion's walls expand to the push of nature. / Mortality yields to sense.' Maguire cannot quite see how this is managed by those around him and his shyness compounds his inability to resolve his sexual desires with the concept of sin. The great sadness at the heart of *The Great Hunger* is well established by the stage of

Kavanagh's anti-pastoral satire against the Irish Literary Revival and its urban tourists in Part XIII.

An idealised view of the Irish peasantry followed the Revival begun by Yeats, Synge and Lady Gregory in the first two decades of the century. Yeats wrote,

> John Synge, I and Augusta Gregory, thought
> All that we did, all that we said or sang
> Must come from contact with the soil.

Kavanagh appears to have had these words in mind when he parodied the travellers' idealisation of the peasant: '*There* is the source from which all cultures rise'. In the passage which follows, the use of the word 'clay' rather than Yeats's 'soil' contrasts Yeats's softer, romantic, general term with the toughness of Maguire's reality in County Monaghan where 'Clay is the word and clay is the flesh'.

This is sharply focused anti-pastoral parody, which is continued to a point where the tone shifts the irony away from the literary establishment's view of Maguire's way of life towards the author's presentation of that life. The travellers' voice comes close to the way Kavanagh has himself presented Maguire when the tourists salute, 'without irony', the peasant's being 'half a vegetable' that nevertheless has the capacity to see 'when the cataract yields'. The peasant's desire for 'conscious joy' and 'intensity' of feeling that are patronised by the travellers are exactly what Kavanagh has had Maguire hungering for. Even the travellers' phrase 'the desire to breed' for the way the peasant views sexual relationships is exactly the way Kavanagh has presented Maguire's view of young girls as 'fillies in season'. Maguire has, indeed, been presented as 'only one remove from the beasts he drives', in the travellers' words.

This is what is ultimately unconvincing about *The Great Hunger* and it is based upon the poem's crucial flaw of pessimistic fatalism.

It is the narrator's voice that says at the end of Part XIII, 'No escape, no escape', although the intention seems to be that this is Maguire's feeling of entrapment. The problem began with the recurring suggestion that Maguire's sense of love was limited to stirrings of animal appetite. This restricts the poet's enquiry into how Maguire becomes alienated from nature by implying, perhaps more than he realises, that Maguire's own nature has not only been repressed and distorted, but is already fundamentally limited. The fatalism that is intended to be in Maguire's mind is actually the poet's attitude towards his subject. In his desire to present Maguire's anguish in a way that avoids heroic alternatives and deflates the pastoral view of the peasant, Kavanagh, like Crabbe, errs on the opposite side. When describing Maguire's death Kavanagh seeks to avoid sub-Yeatsian melodrama: 'No mad hooves galloping in the sky'. But the very image that is most authentic – that of a sick horse seeking a clean place to die – is also unfortunate in again emphasising Maguire's animal nature.

When Kavanagh originally set himself the challenge to present 'an old peasant who can neither be damned nor glorified', he was attempting an impossible neutrality if he really cared about the effects of the Church's distortion of human vitality through its pastoralisation of a 'Nature that never deceives'. The poem's final image of a hunger that screams an 'apocalypse of clay' in the final line, 'In every corner of this land', suggests a metaphor for the state of a national culture that echoes the claim of the poem's title. *The Great Hunger* is a twentieth-century parallel with the anti-pastoral impulse of Goldsmith and Crabbe in having its origins in outrage and compassion, in showing how a nation can alienate its land workers from their inner nature and from the land itself, and in revealing the tensions of a writer caught in the gap between rural authenticity and making a case to an urban readership. The overstraining of language in overstating the case produces a flawed work, but an important one. It should come as no surprise to find that Kavanagh eventually rejected *The Great Hunger* and that his literary career followed the pattern of Duck and Clare in being artistically weakened by acceptance into the literary establishment. In Dublin, John Nemo writes, the Monaghan farmer 'was treated as the literate peasant he had been rather than the highly talented poet he believed he was in the process of becoming' (Nemo 1979: 79). Such a pattern seems to indicate the culture's tendency to pastoralise the anti-pastoral poet.

Such a fate was also unavoidable for those writers of rural non-fiction who sought to speak for the inhabitants of the English countryside whose voice would not otherwise be heard, against the need of the newly urbanised to read pastoral rural writing in the nineteenth and early twentieth centuries. William Cobbett's *Rural Rides* (1830) is now a classic of English rural prose writing, yet what distinguishes it from earlier 'Tours' such as Defoe's of 1722, is its origin in a partisan desire to establish the causes of failing farms and rural poverty in the south of England in the 1820s. As a countryman and small farmer himself at this time, Cobbett's documentation of what he summed up as '*rich land* and *poor labourers*', led to a contempt for those absent aristocratic landowners who neglected their tenants and labourers in urban comfort and, in Cobbett's words,

a gentry, only now-and-then residing at all, having no relish for country-delights, foreign in their manners, distant and haughty in their behaviour, looking to the soil only for its rents, viewing it as a mere object of speculation, unacquainted with its cultivators, despising them and their pursuits, and relying, for influence, not upon the good will of the vicinage, but upon the dread of their power.

Cobbett's moral tenure does not lead, however, to a radically changed future, but to a restoration of past values. In this he is closer to Goldsmith than to Kavanagh.

Cobbett's successor in the latter part of the nineteenth century was Richard Jefferies in his early essays such as *Round about a Great Estate* (1880), which Q. D. Leavis called 'one of the most delightful books in the English language'. In *The Toilers of the Field* (1892) Jefferies says, 'In the life of the English agricultural labourers there is absolutely no poetry, no colour.' He sets out to correct the 'poetical' view of the labourer with a knowing detail astutely used:

> To rise at five of a summer's morning, and see the azure of the sky and the glorious sun, may be, perhaps, no great hardship, although there are few persons who could long remain poetical on bread and cheese. But to rise at five on a dark winter's morning is a very different affair. To put on coarse nailed boots, weighing fully seven pounds, gaiters up above the knee, a short greatcoat of some heavy material, and to step out into the driving rain and trudge wearily over field after field of wet grass, with the furrows full of water; then to sit on a three-legged stool, with mud and manure half-way up the ankles, and milk cows with one's head leaning against their damp, smoking hides for two hours, with the rain coming steadily drip, drip, drip – this is a very different affair.

This is, as W. J. Keith points out, an antidote to 'the sheltered cosiness of most of *Our Village*', Mary Russell Mitford's anodyne sketches from earlier in the century. Jefferies's intention is, like Crabbe's and Cobbett's before him, to seek out '*essential* truth' against urban nostalgia for a rural Arcadia his readers had left behind within living memory. In the later, more lyrical essays, Jefferies is working from memory and he is aware that his own nostalgia may inject more colour than he intends:

> Memory, like the sun, paints to me bright pictures of the golden summer time ... I can see them, but how shall I fix them for you? By no process that can be accomplished. It is like

  a story that cannot be told because he who knows it is tongue-tied and dumb.

The difficulty for the anti-pastoral writer in finding a voice that can be celebratory whilst corrective, that does not adopt the very vices it is criticising, that avoids overstating its case whilst accepting that its case is inevitably a counter one, was solved by Blake in *Songs of Innocence and Experience* (1794) by accepting the dialectic as the mode of writing. He was thus able to celebrate the lamb whilst recognising the 'fearful symmetry' of the need for a celebration of the tiger. By adopting the form of Sunday School homilies, Blake was able both to show the way the sentimentalising pastoral worked and to undercut it to expose the hypocrisy upon which it was based. He was able to give true innocence its importance, whilst indicating the experience required to recognise it. In 'The Garden of Love' from *Experience*, 'A Chapel was built in the midst / Where I used to play on the green.' The 'Thou shalt not, writ over the door' has the effect of 'binding with briars my joys and desires' which, in 'The Echoing Green' in *Experience*, can now be appreciated as communal joys responding to the seasons with desires that are as natural as the flowers. Blake's dialectic demands a return to the *Songs of Innocence* after reading *The Songs of Experience* in order to value the depth of the innocent vision which transcends the sentimental pastoral of their formal origins. The journey through Hell was the way to achieve a perception of Heaven that was not an idealised Arcadia.

Blake's *The Marriage of Heaven and Hell* (*c.* 1793) is his great anti-pastoral work. In it he exposes pastorally-comforting images of Heaven as self-deceiving constructs, what he calls in the poem 'London' from *Experience*, 'the mind-forg'd manacles'. For Blake this is a matter of perception and human choice. As an engraver making his own book in the manner of an artist, Blake again takes his form as the metaphor for his content:

But first the notion that man has a body distinct from his soul is to be expunged. This I shall do by printing in the infernal method by corrosives, which in Hell are salutary and medicinal, melting apparent surfaces away, and displaying the infinite which was hid.

If the doors of perception were cleansed everything would appear to man as it is – infinite.

For man has closed himself up, till he sees all things through narrow chinks of his cavern.

Blake's emphasis is on the self-imprisonment of selective perception. A self-protective tendency has led people to retreat behind the narrow chinks of a cavern of their own making. They are in manacles of their own making that in *Songs of Experience* are 'binding with briars my joys and desires' to such an extent that in the final line of 'London', the evident distortion of desires that leads to the need for the 'harlot', 'blights with plagues the Marriage hearse'.

The inheritor of Blake's vision is Ted Hughes, a poem from whose first collection (1957) appears to be based upon this idea of the pastoral as a selective, self-protective filter. Hughes's 'Egghead' might be representative of what is admired in the partly mad, partly brilliant perceptions of an intellectual. Hughes takes the comic metaphor literally and thinks of the intellectual's skull as a fragile eggshell through which he filters the world and is apparently able to perceive wonders that others cannot. The poem begins with ironic pastoralisms in which nouns are used as decorative adjectives in a seductive-sounding innovation:

A leaf's otherness,
The whaled monstered sea-bottom, eagled peaks
And stars that hang over hurtling endlessness,
  With manslaughtering shocks

Are let in on his sense.

The bathos of 'manslaughtering' indicates that the only shocks which the egghead actually lets in are safely defused by his perception of them. One might expect Hughes's interest to be in the whale or the eagle on the basis of his predatory animal poems such as 'Jaguar', but for the egghead they are reduced to the role of prettifying place ('eagled peaks'), to the extent that they 'are let in' at all by his filter. The ironic tone is continued in:

> So many a one has dared to be struck dead
> Peeping through his fingers at the world's ends,
>   Or at an ant's head.

In 'Egghead' the logic of 'prudently' excluding uncomfortable natural forces is ultimately self-destructive since the forces themselves will not be suppressed by being ignored. 'The whelm of the sun' and 'the bolt of the earth' are potentially destructive as well as creative forces. This egg's chemistry of complacency and arrogance hatches a man/cockerel who 'trumpet[s] his own ear dead' in the poem's rather overstraining final lines. The strange vehemence of this ending also has something in common with Blake's choice of corrosives for a 'salutary' cleansing purpose.

In his first two collections, Ted Hughes wrote poems which celebrated natural forces through 'cleansed' perceptions (such as 'Crow Hill'), together with anti-pastoral poems which exposed self-deceptive constructions of nature (such as 'Thrushes'). But the opportunity to undercut idealisations of nature is taken in every one of his major collections. At the time of the death of Ted Hughes, John Carey wrote in the *Sunday Times* (1 November 1998), 'Pastoral poetry, in Hughes's hands, acquires an armoury of new warheads'. The poem 'Glimpse' in *Crow* (1970) tells how Crow's trembling lyric about the leaves is cut short by 'the touch of a leaf's edge at his throat'. But for the mischievous Crow one lesson is not enough, and the need for the comfort of a pastoral vision is hard to stop:

Speechless he continued to stare at the leaves

Through the god's head instantly substituted.

In *Cave Birds* (1978) the pastoral idyll of the earth as 'a busy hive of heavens' in 'A Green Mother' includes 'the heaven of the worm' where the dead protagonist will be processed: 'Little of you will be rejected – / Which the angels of the flowers will gladly collect'.

The most striking evidence that Hughes adopted Blake's corrosive method is in his public readings from *Moortown Diary* (1979), a collection of poems from a period of farming. Hughes has written,

> The bulk of these pieces, I'm aware, concern the nursing if not the emergency hospital side of animal husbandry. All sheep, lambs and calves are patients: something in them all is making a steady effort to die. That is the farmer's impression.

This last sentence indicates that Hughes is mediating for a non-farming readership. Some of these poems describe horrific farming procedures. At every opportunity Hughes read the poem 'February 17th' in which a lamb, strangled in the process of being born, has to have its head cut off in order to save the mother. I have seen people faint in the audience at readings of this poem. On a commercial tape Hughes defends himself thus:

> Once I read this in a hall full of university students and one member of the audience rebuked me for reading what he called 'a disgusting piece of horror writing'. We either have a will to examine what happens or we have a will to evade it.

Cosy associations with lambs persist, but only an anti-pastoral propagandist would continue to cleanse with a corrosive text like 'February 17th' in the spirit of Thomas Hardy's dictum: 'If way to the Better there be, / It behoves a full look at the Worst'.

Christopher Marlowe actually used the phrase 'pretty Lambes' in his classic pastoral of 1600, 'The passionate Sheepheard to his love', which was the subject of an early English anti-pastoral satire. Marlowe's poem famously begins:

Come live with mee, and be my love,
And we will all the pleasures prove,
That Vallies, groves, hills and fieldes,
Woods, or steepie mountaine yeeles.

And wee will sit upon the Rocks,
Seeing the Sheepheards feede theyr flocks,
By shallow Rivers, to whose falls,
Melodius byrds sing Madrigalls.

The idea that the birds around them sing madrigals might amuse contemporary shepherds distributing their EEC subsidised feed. The idea amused Sir Walter Ralegh enough for him to write 'The Nimphs reply to the Sheepheard' (1600), an imitation of the form and a corrective of the contents of Marlowe's poem:

If all the world and love were young,
And truth in every Sheepheards tongue,
These pretty pleasures might me move,
To live with thee, and be thy love.

Time drives the flocks from field to fold,
When Rivers rage, and Rocks grow cold,
And Philomell becommeth dombe,
The rest complaines of cares to come.

The flowers doe fade, and wanton fieldes,
To wayward winter reckoning yeeldes,
A honny tongue, a hart of gall,
Is fancies spring, but sorrowes fall.

The clinching final line here is a typical undercutting of the literary convention upon which the pastoral is based – it is a fancy usually played out in the spring – by a realism that forces a return to hard judgements about what is 'a honny tongue' and what a sincere celebration of natural beauty. The cynicism of Raleigh's position in his poem is to deny any possibility that love could last through a 'winter reckoning'.

This problem lies at the heart of all anti-pastoral satire. Byron typically encourages the notion that his epic poem *Don Juan* (1819) is based upon cynicism when he announces the theme and setting for his poem: 'What men call gallantry, and gods adultery, / Is much more common where the climate's sultry.' His young hero is seduced by a married woman and Byron seems to be satirising a figure like Marlowe's shepherd in describing the pastoral mode of the boy's reciprocal love:

> He pored upon the leaves, and on the flowers,
>   And heard a voice in all the winds; and then
> He thought of wood nymphs and immortal bowers,
>   And how the goddesses came down to men:
> He miss'd the pathway, he forgot the hours,
>   And when he look'd upon his watch again,
> He found how much old Time had been a winner –
> He also found that he had lost his dinner.

After the almost Elizabethan notion of 'old Time' as 'winner' – that last word sounding a subtle warning, perhaps, that this is not quite Elizabethan – the bathos of the final line punches home the satire.

It is the momentum of Byron's satire in his use of his invented form, ottava rima, that carries the impact of his poetic dexterity. In four stanzas in particular his target is not just Wordsworth, but a kind of metaphysical nature poetry that includes pastoral enquiry such as Jaques's in *As You Like It*. His point of attack is the pretension of what can become too abstract, self-centred and obscuring its intention, together with the 'learned' artifice upon which the mode is based:

> Young Juan wander'd by the glassy brooks
>   Thinking unutterable things; he threw
> Himself at length within the leafy nooks
>   Where the wild branch of the cork forest grew;
> There poets find material for their books,
>   And every now and then we read them through,
> So that their plan and prosody are eligible,
> Unless, like Wordsworth, they prove unintelligible.
>
> He, Juan (and not Wordsworth) so pursued
>   His self-communion with his own high soul,
> Until his mighty heart, in its great mood,
>   Had mitigated part, though not the whole
> Of its disease; he did the best he could
>   With things not very subject to control,
> And turn'd, without perceiving his condition,
> Like Coleridge, into a metaphysician.
>
> He thought about himself, and the whole earth,
>   Of man the wonderful, and of the stars,
> And how the deuce they ever could have birth;
>   And then he thought of earthquakes, and of wars,
> How many miles the moon might have in girth,
>   Of air-balloons, and of the many bars
> To perfect knowledge of the boundless skies;
> And then he thought of Donna Julia's eyes.
>
> In thoughts like these true wisdom may discern
>   Longings sublime, and aspirations high,
> Which some are born with, but the most part learn
>   To plague themselves withal, they know not why:

'Twas strange that one so young should thus concern
  His brain about the action of the sky;
 If *you* think 'twas philosophy that this did,
 I can't help thinking puberty assisted.

The real irony of all this is that Byron is himself a superb nature poet who can use imagery of place to evoke the complex emotions of his characters, although outside the conventions of the pastoral. He cannot take himself seriously enough to adopt a literary convention 'to plague [himself] withal'. What we are left with in this section of *Don Juan* is a challenge to our reading of pastoral, once again demanding a discrimination of the self-deceptive and escapist, from that which offers insights upon return.

Perhaps the most successful equivalent of this anti-pastoral satire in the novel is Stella Gibbons's *Cold Comfort Farm* (1932), which targets the rural novels of Mary Webb and T. F. Powys, with perhaps a glance at Hardy and Lawrence whose strengths are sufficient defence against parody. In order to appreciate the effect of Stella Gibbons's anti-pastoral it is necessary to juxtapose a passage from Mary Webb with one from *Cold Comfort Farm*. Here is the full paragraph from *Gone to Earth* (1917) which was referred to in the outline of rural fiction in Chapter 3. Webb is describing the way Andrew is connected to the natural environment of Undern:

> But to Undern itself he was not indifferent. Ties deep as the tangled roots of the bindweed, strong as the great hawsers of the beeches that reached below the mud of Undern Pool, held him to it, the bondslave of a beauty he could not understand, a terror he could not express. When he trudged the muddy paths, 'setting taters' or earthing up; when he scythed the lawn, looking, with a rose in his hat, weirder and more ridiculous than ever; and when he shook the apples down with a kind of sour humour, as if to say, 'There! that's what you trees get by having

apples!' – at all these times he seemed less an individual than a blind force. For though his personality was strong, that of the place was stronger. Half out of the soil, minded like the dormouse and the beetle, he was, by virtue of his unspoken passion, the protoplasm of a poet.

Quite what it is to be 'the protoplasm of a poet' is hard to grasp. But that's the point: the mystery of Andrew's mind is that it is half in the soil and cannot comprehend the beauty and terror of which he is strangely part.

Here is Stella Gibbons's Adam:

From the stubborn interwoven strata of his subconscious, thought seeped up into his dim conscious; not as an integral part of that consciousness, but more as an impalpable emanation, a crepuscular addition, from the unsleeping life in the restless trees and fields surrounding him. The country for miles, under the blanket of the dark which brought no peace, was in its annual tortured ferment of spring growth; worm jarred with worm and seed with seed. Frond leapt on frond and hare on hare. Beetle and finch-fly were not spared. The trout sperm in the muddy hollow under Nettle Flitch Weir were agitated, and well they might be. The long screams of the hunting owls tore across the night, scarlet lines on black. In the pauses, every ten minutes, they mated. It seemed chaotic, but it was more methodically arranged than you might think. But Adam's deafness and blindness came from within, as well as without; earthly calm seeped up from his subconscious and met descending calm in his conscious.

Whilst the parodic references to the unconscious might echo from Lawrence, the sense of Andrew's 'blind force' in the 'unsleeping life' of Adam is as unmistakable as the 'tortured ferment' here is as a parody of the beauty and terror in Mary Webb's construction of nature.

One of the most recent anti-pastoral texts is Tom Stoppard's 1993 play *Arcadia*. It is actually a satire about academics who make their careers by researching the pastoral. The play takes place in a room giving on to the garden of a Derbyshire stately home and the scenes alternate between 1809 and the present. In 1809 the gardens are about to be redesigned by the landscape architect, Noakes, in the manner of the picturesque. Noakes has made a book showing the garden before and after his changes. Lady Croom, the owner of Sidley Park, does not approve of the new fashion:

> Here is the Park as it appears to us now, and here as it might be when Mr Noakes has done with it. Where there is the familiar pastoral refinement of an Englishman's garden, here is an eruption of gloomy forest and towering crag, of ruins where there was never a house, of water dashing against rocks where there was neither spring nor a stone I could not throw the length of a cricket pitch. My hyacinth dell is become a haunt for hobgoblins, my Chinese bridge, which I am assured is superior to the one at Kew, and for all I know at Peking, is usurped by a fallen obelisk overgrown with briars.

We watch Lady Croom's thirteen year-old daughter, Thomasina, paint a hermit in Noakes's sketchbook to inhabit the proposed hermitage. The modern researcher of early nineteenth-century history, Hannah Jarvis, assuming that there was a real hermit whose papers were found in the hermitage (in reality Thomasina's mathematical experiments), explains to her rival academic the thesis she is building around the hermit's flawed genius:

HANNAH: Peacock says he was suspected of genius. It turned out, of course, he was off his head. He'd covered every sheet with cabalistic proofs that the world was coming to an end. It's perfect, isn't it? A perfect symbol, I mean.
BERNARD: Oh, yes. Of what?

> HANNAH: The whole Romantic sham, Bernard! It's what happened to the Enlightenment, isn't it? A century of intellectual rigour turned in on itself. A mind in chaos suspected of genius. In a setting of cheap thrills and false emotion. The history of the garden says it all, beautifully. There's an engraving of Sidley Park in 1730 that makes you want to weep. Paradise in the age of reason. By 1760 everything had gone – the topiary, pools and terraces, fountains, an avenue of limes – the whole sublime geometry was ploughed under by Capability Brown. The grass went from the doorstep to the horizon and the best box hedge in Derbyshire was dug up for the ha-ha so that the fools could pretend they were living in God's countryside. And then Richard Noakes came in to bring God up to date. By the time he'd finished it looked like this (*the sketch book*). The decline from thinking to feeling, you see.

Hannah's simplistic thesis is undermined not only by her believing that the garden prior to 1730 was 'paradise', but by the audience's knowledge that the 'cabalistic proofs' are really a thirteen-year-old girl's mathematics. This potted history of landscape design serves to remind the audience that Arcadia is a social construct of each age. The present Arcadian construct, the play suggests, might be a mathematical model of the universe. Thomasina's papers turn out to have anticipated a way of representing the essence of each part of nature as a mathematical object. This current theory is displacing the previous fashion for physics, explains Valentine, an Oxford post-graduate student of biology: 'People were talking about the end of physics. Relativity and quantum looked as if they were going to clean out the whole problem between them.' But, 'the problem turns out to be different'. So Valentine's enthusiasm for approaching the mysteries of the universe in a new way is offered, in the context of the play, as just another Arcadian construct, even though it cleverly tries to take account of the 'noise' of the unpredictable, that is 'people fancying people who aren't supposed to be in that part of the plan', as the modern daughter of the house puts it.

Stoppard's strongest satire is reserved for the self-proclaimed 'Media Don' whose false discovery of Byron's having shot a minor poet in a duel at Sidley Park will be challenged by Hannah in a letter to the *Times*. In the elegant writing and dramatic wit of this play Stoppard is himself impressively Byronic. But Stoppard's cynicism is embedded in the structure of the play, which suggests through parallel characters and relationships that events are merely repeating themselves. His suggestion that conceptions of nature, whether in landscape, architecture or in scientific theories, are fashionable Arcadias in a continuum which also includes some repetition, is given dramatic form at the end of the play when the characters from the two periods are in the room together and appear to be making continuous sense in their parallel conversations:

> VALENTINE: And everything is mixing the same way, all the time, irreversibly . . .
>
> SEPTIMUS: Oh, we have time, I think.
>
> VALENTINE: . . . till there's no time left. That's what time means.
>
> SEPTIMUS: When we have found all the mysteries and lost all the meaning, we will be alone, on an empty shore.

And so Septimus, the tutor of 1809, anticipates the bleak image of the loss of meaning in the universe created so devastatingly by Matthew Arnold in 'Dover Beach'.

Stoppard's modern notion of the closed circuit of the pastoral continuum, expressed in a work that is itself a part of an anti-pastoral continuum, raises the question of whether it is possible to perceive any literature as having broken out of the circle of idealisation and its corrective, a literature that might be characterised as 'post-pastoral', not in its chronology but in its conceptions.

6

POST-PASTORAL

In offering, in the first chapter, three uses of the term pastoral, the intention was to clarify three general strands of usage – the literary convention, literature of the countryside and the pejorative of idealisation – rather than to make firm definitive distinctions. It will now be realised how much these strands can overlap in that a travel book about Antarctica by Sara Wheeler, *Terra Incognita* (1996), might be called a pastoral work in all three senses: she views Antarctica as an Arcadia from which to return with a renewed sense of herself; it is a travelogue describing a natural environment; it could be regarded as an escapist pastoral that self-indulgently ignores, or touches too lightly upon, the urgent political issues concerning the exploitation of the continent. Indeed, 'the pastoral's multiple frames', as Lawrence Buell puts it, can now be seen to include not only a range of kinds of pastoral, but the way in which a single text may be read within several frames. 'More often than not', Buell says of American pastorals, 'accommodation and reformism are interfused' (Buell 1995: 52). *The Winter's Tale* might posit alternative values in the location of retreat, but must ultimately accommodate its contemporary court audience if it is to be staged at all. Similarly Leo Marx's 'pastoral of sentiment and pastoral of the mind' might not be so easily distinguished in the case of Wordsworth's 'Michael' with which this book began. This is not a case in which, as Marx claims, 'the pastoral design, as always, circumscribes the pastoral ideal' (Marx 1964: 72). Wordsworth believes his idyll to represent the truth of human interrelatedness with nature.

But even in putting it this way, we are reading Wordsworth's texts in a way pastoral has not been read before. Ecocriticism may be the frame of our age, informed with a new kind of concern for 'environment', rather than 'countryside' or 'landscape' or the 'bucolic', but we cannot pretend that there have not been changes in our knowledge, attitudes and ideology. We cannot pretend that the relationship between texts referring to nature and urbanised readers (who may live in villages but be economically orientated towards the urban) has not changed. And despite Buell's complaint that the pastoral 'has been treated with much astringency of late' (Buell 1995: 33), we cannot ignore both the evidence of the anti-pastoral and the development of the pejorative use of the term in twentieth-century British culture. That the pastoral has become not only a 'contested term', but a deeply suspect one, is the cultural position in which we find ourselves.

Yet the pastoral impulse of retreat and return persists in writing about nature. This is what Buell calls 'pastoralism' when he makes this claim at the beginning of his book *The Environmental Imagination*:

> Insofar as some form of pastoralism is part of the conceptual apparatus of all persons with western educations interested in leading more nature-sensitive lives, it is to be expected that pastoralism will be part of the unavoidable ground-condition of most of those who read this book. Even if, as is clear, pastoralism interposes some major stumbling blocks in the way

of developing a mature environmental aesthetics, it cannot but play a major role in that endeavor.

(Buell 1995: 32)

The stumbling-blocks of our current position have just been described and they demand more than to be glossed over so easily. But the contemporary pursuit of 'a mature environmental aesthetics', with all its dangers of just being another form of landscape construction as Tom Stoppard might suggest – yet another era's Arcadia – has gathered a forceful critique of the pastoral mode that is aware of its relativism, of the choices available, of its honourable and its dishonourable traditions. 'A mature environmental aesthetics' would need to recognise that some literature has gone beyond the closed circuit of pastoral and anti-pastoral to achieve a vision of an integrated natural world that includes the human. Buell is himself part of this new movement that seeks to define a pastoral that has avoided the traps of idealisation in seeking to find a discourse that can both celebrate *and* take some responsibility for nature without false consciousness. Indeed, Buell describes the most recent shift in contemporary pastoral ideology as the development of ecocriticism, in which he plays a leading part:

As this ecocentric repossession of pastoral has gathered force, its center of energy has begun to shift from representation of nature as a theater for human events to representation in the sense of advocacy of nature as a presence for its own sake.

(Buell 1995: 52)

This is, in effect, a reversal of focus in the elements of the pastoral. Now we have as much an interest in the welfare of Arden as in that of its exiled inhabitants, as much interest in their interaction with Arden as in what they take back from it, as much interest in how they represent their interaction with it as in how their representations of themselves as its inhabitants have changed.

In ecocritical readings, the court is not the real world but the literary convention. Arden, the literary convention, now stands for the real world we inhabit. Ecocritical readings seek images of what might be called, in answer to Lear, 'accommodated man', at home in the natural world as much as in the social world.

What is needed is a new term to refer to literature that is aware of the anti-pastoral and of the conventional illusions upon which Arcadia is premised, but which finds a language to outflank those dangers with a vision of accommodated humans, at home in the very world they thought themselves alienated from by their possession of language. Such a term should enable 'a mature environmental aesthetics' to sift the 'sentimental pastoral' from the 'complex pastoral' in a way which takes account of the urgent need for responsibility and, indeed, advocacy for the welfare of Arden, informed by our current and updated best judgements of what that should be. Just as ecocriticism is interdisciplinary in drawing from scientific reports on global and regional environmental issues (see *State of the World* published annually by W. W. Norton), from philosophy and environmental ethics (see Abram 1996 and Foster 1997), from theoretical debates about language and representation (see Scigaj 1996 and 1999), and from artistic engagements with these issues other than in literature (see Gifford 1996 on the paintings of Julian Cooper), so a term for literature that addresses the problems of human accommodation with nature should be able to encompass visionaries from the past as well as the present and a range of forms from the ballad to travel writing. The linguistic assumptions of such a term would be those set out by Leonard M. Scigaj in an essay suggesting that against the postmodern notion of language as constantly deferring meaning based upon the shades of difference between words, Derrida's *différance*, in order to discuss environmental degradation we need to see language as actually pointing outwards to material reality. Scigaj calls this *référance*, 'the referential origin of all language' (Scigaj 1996: 6). When Gerard Manley Hopkins refers to the 'soil' in a poem about what we have done to it, however many poetic reverberations the word might have in our culture, we had better believe that we cannot constantly defer our responsibility for our degradation of a real material upon which our lives depend. Manley Hopkins's poetry is ultimately a literature demanding our re-examination of our real daily relationship with 'soil', whether we regard it as 'God's Grandeur', as he does in his poem's title, or not.

Elsewhere I have proposed the term 'post-pastoral' for such literature and defined it by six qualities in the poetry of Ted Hughes (Gifford 1995: 121*ff*). I now want to elaborate those six constituents of a definition, with some changes, by reference, for each one, to both the work of a poet and the work of a prose writer. This will risk appearing to be making some crude separations and distinctions of notions which are more subtle in their contexts and more interdependent in practice, but that is a risk inherent in the explication of any literary tool. Suffice it to say that all six qualities cannot be expected to be present in every text of a post-pastoral writer and will be found together in one remarkable text only rarely, but they will all be a part of the vision represented in the best work of a post-pastoral writer. Many of these elements in the post-pastoral construction of the human relationship with nature have their origins in aspects of the traditions of pastoral and anti-pastoral literature. It should therefore be no surprise to find familiar names appearing here in the clarification of a certain quality that goes towards making the holistic vision of the post-pastoral. Some writers, such as Wordsworth, Heaney or Hughes, are capable of writing, at different times, pastoral, anti-pastoral and post-pastoral texts. Within Wordsworth's 'Home at Grasmere' one might read different passages as pastoral, anti-pastoral or post-pastoral. Compare, for example, this classic pastoral retreat:

> Delightful Valley, habitation fair!
> And to whatever else of outward form
> Can give us inward help, can purify,

> And elevate, and harmonize, and soothe,
> And steal away, and for a while deceive
> And lap in pleasing rest, and bear us on
> Without desire in full complacency,
> Contemplating perfection absolute
> And entertained as in a placid sleep.

with this explicit denial of 'all Arcadian dreams':

> Give entrance to the sober truth; avow
> That Nature to this favourite Spot of ours
> Yields no exemption, but her awful rights
> Enforces to the utmost and exacts
> Her tribute of inevitable pain,
> And that the sting is added, man himself
> For ever busy to afflict himself.

with the most profound post-pastoral discovery (quoted in the previous chapter),

> of nothing more than what we are –
> How exquisitely the individual Mind
> (And the progressive powers perhaps no less
> Of the whole species) to the external world
> Is fitted; and how exquisitely too –
> Theme this but little heard of among men –
> The external world is fitted to the mind.

A final caveat ought to be added: that the six elements suggested here are probably capable of further elaboration, or elision, so that readers might want to expand my definition to twelve elements or reduce it to three. So with these qualifications in mind, let me attempt an outline of what might begin to constitute the 'more mature environmental aesthetics' that Buell suggests is our moment's urgently needed development in a literary criticism that has its roots firmly in 'the pastoral's multiple frames'.

Fundamental to post-pastoral literature is an awe in attention to the natural world. Such a respect derives not just from a naturalist's intimate knowledge or a modern ecologist's observation of the dynamics of relationships, but from a deep sense of the immanence in all natural things. It is not surprising that a good example of awe is at the centre of the work of a religious poet such as Gerard Manley Hopkins. His poem, 'God's Grandeur' (1918), exemplifies the way this positioning of the self towards nature leads inevitably to a humbling that is a necessary requirement of the shift from the anthropocentric position of the pastoral to the ecocentric view of the post-pastoral. The poem's first stanza ends by deploring the results of anthropocentrism:

> And all is seared with trade; bleared, smeared with toil;
> And wears man's smudge and shares man's smell: the soil
> Is bare now, nor can foot feel, being shod.

In three lines Hopkins evokes four of the five senses to show the physical, elemental cost of human exploitative alienation from the earth. Importantly the next stanza begins: 'And for all this, nature is never spent; / There lives the dearest freshness deep down things.' Hopkins's condensed grammar strains, like Wordsworth's, to express the fierce intensity and complexity that lies behind the simple word 'awe'.

There is a sense in which the role of the land and the weather in the novels of Cormac McCarthy induces a similar humbling awe in the reader, albeit from a writer who might appear to be very different from the author of 'God's Grandeur'. McCarthy's bleak vision is in direct contrast to the joyous celebration of this poem. But when one remembers that Hopkins is also the author of the desperately anguished sonnet 'No worst, there is none', one might think of Hopkins as a New Testament teacher and doubter, whilst

McCarthy adopts the tone of an Old Testament chronicler. The role of rain in *The Crossing* (1994), for example, at two points acts as an impressive humbling force outside of human control or comprehension. In the first, it is a wall of water into which two horsemen ride 'and are wet instantly'. They dismount and stand under a grove of trees 'and watched the rain roar in the mud'. Neither of them comments and, although they are drenched and it is now night, they mount up and ride on, still, the reader knows, suffering but surviving a strangely belittling trial. At another point, awe at the way rain can fall on one side of the white line down a road and not the other is the subject of a conversation that unifies two men in their shared incomprehension. It is the distance of McCarthy's style that gives these moments significance through their understatement. In the final sentence of this novel McCarthy is explicit about the role of land and weather for his characters since he uses the preacher-influenced language of his characters to describe it: 'He sat there for a long time and after a while the east did gray and after a while the right and godmade sun did rise, once again, for all and without distinction.' This last phrase appears negative in its tone, but it has the effect of unifying humbled humans with their environment in the face of cycles of elemental power.

The second fundamental aspect of the post-pastoral is the recognition of a creative–destructive universe equally in balance in a continuous momentum of birth and death, death and rebirth, growth and decay, ecstasy and dissolution. Often this requires a recognition of the death process, as it does for Coleridge's Ancient Mariner who had not learned humility before the huge presence of the Albatross and had committed the hubris of causing the arbitrary death of not just the only fellow creature in the ice and fog, but one welcomed 'As if it had been a Christian soul'. The reader senses that the anthropocentricity of this act will need some radical adjustment if the Mariner is to appease his crime against nature. He will need to recognise the independent souls of all creatures, including those that horrify him as 'slimy things [that] crawl with legs / Upon the slimy sea'. It was when he saw their intrinsic beauty that, 'A spring of love gushed from my heart, / And I blessed them unaware.' The spontaneous blessing of the water-snakes is an acceptance of death within life that is the opposite of 'the Nightmare Life-in-Death' the Mariner had earlier witnessed. The profundity of this experience eludes the powers of expression of the Mariner who can only sum it up in the homily 'He prayeth best, who loveth best / All things both great and small.' But the Wedding-Guest has taken in the impact of the tale – 'He went like one that hath been stunned' – which has been told in order to counterbalance a wedding. One might see this dramatic paradox as the equivalent of the seventeenth-century painter's inclusion of an inscription on a tomb in a wood: 'Et in Arcadia Ego' – 'Even in Arcadia, I (Death) am here.' This Latin reminder of the presence of the death process within the most idyllic creative context is best known from the French painter Poussin's *The Arcadian Shepherds* (painted 1629–30 and in the Duke of Devonshire's collection at Chatsworth), although its first representation is in a painting of the same title made six years earlier by the Italian Giovanni Francesco Guercino (Panofsky 1970: 350). The Mariner's mysterious tale of the need to love the death process also is symbolically framed by a marriage.

Perhaps the most penetrating explorations of the cycles and tensions of the dynamics of the creative–destructive universe are to be found in the work of Blake, D. H. Lawrence and Ted Hughes. But the nature writing of John Muir (1838–1914), the Scottish-born founding father of the American conservation movement and inventor of National Parks, provides an interesting example of the difficulty of maintaining the creative–destructive tension in balance without distortion. Muir was the first person who might be said to have taken Coleridge's vision the first step along the road to legislation. Roderick Nash, in *The Rights of Nature*, says that Muir was the first person in America to accord rights to other creatures, significantly snakes and alligators. Muir's Puritanical father was keen to spot 'the work of the Devil' and John Muir will have been left in no doubt that the serpent was an unequivocal symbol of evil. (Coleridge was, of course, drawing upon this Christian symbolism in creating his image of the water-snakes.) But in John Muir's posthumous book, *A Thousand Mile Walk to the Gulf* (1916) he has this remarkable passage:

> The antipathies existing in the Lord's great animal family must be wisely planned, like balanced repulsion and attraction in the mineral kingdom. How narrow we selfish, conceited creatures are in our sympathies! how blind to the rights of the rest of all creation! . . . Though alligators, snakes, etc., naturally repel us, they are not mysterious evils. They dwell happily in these flowery wilds, are part of God's family, unfallen, undepraved, and cared for.
>
> (Gifford 1992: 148)

To Muir all nature is dynamic, living in 'balanced repulsion and attraction', and his favourite image for this is 'flowing'. In his most famous book, *My First Summer in the Sierra* (1911), he wrote: 'Contemplating the lace-like fabric of streams outspread over the mountains, we are reminded that everything is flowing – going somewhere, animals and so-called lifeless rocks as well as water.' John Muir knew that trees are travellers because he climbed a tree in a storm to experience its 'travels'; he knew that 'mountains are constantly walking', in Gary Snyder's translation of the Chinese proverb (Snyder 1992: 98), and he proved that ice was still flowing by his measurement of active glaciers in the Sierra Nevada mountains of California. In the last book he wrote, *Travels in Alaska* (1915), Muir wrote of the destructive forces of the great glaciers of Alaska as, in effect, creative energies shaping a beautiful landscape: 'Out of all the cold darkness and glacial crushing and grinding comes this warm abounding beauty and life to teach us that what we in our faithless ignorance and fear call destruction is creation finer and finer.' There is a danger in Muir's otherwise post-pastoral writing, of not giving full acknowledgement to the death process in his desire to emphasise the positive part everything has to play in the proto-ecological vision of nature contained in his writing. To say 'all destruction is really creation' is to come close to reverting to pastoral complacency in the face of the realities of decay, ageing, illness and death. The taking and giving of the ecological process inevitably involves some losses and some gains, some pain and some joy in what, for example, Ted Hughes calls the 'epic poise' of the salmon's movement towards procreation and death.

One of the ways we come to terms with this in our own species is by learning that what is happening in us is paralleled in external nature. This third feature of the post-pastoral is the recognition that the inner is also the workings of the outer, that our inner human nature can be understood in relation to external nature. When we have accepted the need for humility as a species we can regain our place as part of the natural world – distinctively human but able to comprehend our humanity through what David Abram calls 'the recuperation of the incarnate, sensorial dimension of experience [which] brings with it a recuperation of the living landscape in which we are corporeally embedded' (Abram 1996: 65). It has been known for some time that people who live beside a tree or with a cat, or tend a garden or a horse, gain some sense of themselves, of their own cycles of growth and decay, and of their emotional ebbs and flows that are unavailable to the inhabitants of concrete tower blocks. The evidence for this in the culture accumulates daily in such reports as one which pointed out that hospital patients need less medication and are discharged earlier if they are opposite a window facing a tree rather than a brick wall. In *The Living Landscape* (1986) Fraser Harrison has described how living in the cycles of a landscape 'offers the most accessible and emotive representation of our own biological fate'.

When Lawrence Buell suggested that 'Muir never seriously considered that the "pathetic fallacy" might be fallacious', he was drawing attention to the basis for all nature imagery. Buell continued, 'Among all the great American nature writers, he was the most striking case of spontaneous pantheism' (Buell 1995: 192). Muir knew that the life in natural things was on a continuum with the life inside ourselves that is 'infinite' in Blake's sense. To say that a willow tree is 'weeping' is to see into the natural characteristic of the tree that is often 'perished at the heart' as the medieval carol 'The Bitter Withy' puts it (Lloyd 1967: 124). In this remarkable song the final evocation of the willow tree somehow represents the song's accumulated anguish of the Christ child at the hands of playground bullies, of his mother in dealing with a child who has miraculous powers, of his own temptation to revenge, of the mothers of the posh bullies whom he drowns, and of his own pain from the caning his mother gives him with 'withy twigs'. The tree which is always to be seen 'perished at the heart' in the English countryside, is now a living totem of the complex of events and emotions that has led to its having suffered, in this remarkable song, this curse of Christ. The pre-literate poets of the folksongs knew that the continuum between external nature in the willow, or the rose, and our internal nature could be used to understand some aspects of our deepest and most complex experiences such as suffering, or love, for example, in 'The Seeds of Love' :

> For in June there's a red rose bud
> And that's the flower for me,
> But I pulled and I plucked
> At that red rose bud
> And I gained the willow tree
> And I gained the willow tree.

Of course, such complex human emotions cannot be fully accounted for by this imagery. Sorley MacLean, the rationalist

Gaelic poet, says at the end of 'The Woods of Raasay', 'the way of the sap is known' to science, but 'There is no knowledge of the course / of the crooked veering of the heart'. Yet to describe those veerings as 'crooked' like a tree's crooked growth is to have already a partial apprehension that such 'veerings' are entirely natural.

Peter Redgrove, a trained scientist who is a poet, novelist and playwright, has built a literary career out of exploring the implications of Wordsworth's discovery that the mind is our tool 'exquisitely fitted' to understand our interactive life in nature. Redgrove's access to the mind is through our dreams' connection with our lost animal sixth sense of 'extra-sensuous perception'. Redgrove's work explores how the inner cycles and veerings of our moods are linked to changes in invisible natural forces such as air pressure, residual electricity and gravitation pulls, for example. But because his access to these forces is through the imagery of dreams, his poetry suffers from making dream-like connections between internal and external nature that are difficult to extrapolate. Redgrove has said that 'the text of nature' cannot be expected to offer 'just a single meaning . . . Rather it is an expanding riddle of a multiplicity of resonating images'. Neil Roberts, in his study of Redgrove's *œuvre*, suggests that one way to read the poetry is to understand that the writer 'is not an onlooker, externally in command of the world and experience' (Roberts 1994: 16). The result is a post-pastoral poet who has dissolved the distinctions between inner and outer nature in such a way as to produce 'resonating riddles' with carnivalesque delight.

Gillian Clarke's poem 'The Hare' (*Letting in the Rumour* 1989) is an implicit endorsement of Redgrove's belief that female experience tends to link the inner and the outer more than male experience is allowed to do by its conventional social construction. It is the failure to draw from the feminine aspects of themselves that is the tragedy of the macho heroes in Cormac McCarthy's novels and is the reason why Billy Parham is crying at the end of *The Crossing* (1994). Doing what he thought his father would have done has led Billy, in this novel, to fail to pay sufficient attention to caring for his brother who is now dead as a consequence. Gillian Clarke's poem is dedicated to her fellow poet Frances Horovitz, who died of cancer in 1983. In this poem the two poets, in a silent cottage at night, hear the cry of a hare, caught in a trap perhaps, which they had both immediately mistaken as a baby's cry. The darkness in which they had felt calmly at ease now contains terrible suffering, anticipating the suffering of Frances Horovitz whose memory, Clarke says at the end of the poem, 'can calm me still'. This duality is held, in the final images of the poem, to offer icons of understanding for that calm and that death: 'the cattle / asleep under a full moon' and 'the stiffening body of the hare'. The image of the full moon refers back to a personal link between the two women established earlier in the poem by the 'sisterly lunacy' of their shared 'phases of the moon'. This, in turn, is associated with the references to mothering in the poem that come to a climax in the poignant lines about Francis Horovitz continuing to menstruate even as she was dying of cancer. Thus the poem reverberates beyond the moving personal relationship of two women who are actually 'Different / as earth and air', to recognise that the dualities of calmness and suffering, and of mothering and dying, are woven not only within female experience but in the whole of nature. This continuity enables another Welsh poet, Christine Evans, in her book *Cometary Phases* (1989), to understand another stage of mothering – letting go of her son – by reference to external nature in the devastatingly simple line, 'Once core, I grow towards husk'.

John Ruskin knew that the outer shaped the development of the inner and much of his work was concerned to examine and explain the way this could happen most effectively to the benefit of the inner. He also sought, in his role as a major influence in the formation of the National Trust, to benefit the preservation of external nature too. 'God has lent us the earth', he wrote in 1849, 'for our life; it is a great entail. It belongs as much to those who come after us . . . as to us.' The reason for Ruskin's concern to respond to this 'entail' – that is, a legal responsibility for an inheritance – is founded upon his belief that the character of a people is determined by their experience of their part of the earth, its climate, geology, topography, flora and fauna. Indeed, the very title of Ruskin's Chapter XVII in *Modern Painters Volume III*, 'The Moral of Landscape', indicates how deeply the internal nature of humans was influenced by their external nature, in his view. Against the fashion in education for 'the destruction of the love of nature' in favour of 'the abstract sciences', Ruskin argued that 'its presence is an invariable sign of goodness of heart and justness of moral perception':

> Instead of supposing the love of nature necessarily connected with the faithlessness of the age, I believe it is connected properly with the benevolence and liberty of the age; that it is precisely the most healthy element which distinctively belongs to us; and that out of it, cultivated no longer in levity or ignorance, but in earnestness and as a duty, results will spring of an importance at present inconceivable; and lights arise, which, for the first time in man's history, will reveal to him the true nature of his life, the true field for his energies, and the true relations between him and his Maker.

For Ruskin there was an inevitable separation between nature and culture, however closely culture reconnected humans' inner nature with external nature. The gendered history of this separation is summed up in Sherry B. Ortner's famous essay title 'Is Female to Male as Nature Is to Culture?' (Rosaldo and Lamphere 1974: 86) This is an anthropologist's analysis and the biological basis for this historical construct is the subject of much debate within ecofeminism. Carolyn Merchant's history of science describing the linking of women and nature by male scientists since the Renaissance was referred to in Chapter 1. Our art, on the other hand, may be a mode of feeling our way back into a balanced relationship with external nature. The American poet Gary Snyder has suggested that culture *is* nature, that our art is our natural way of thinking ourselves back into the natural world from which much of our previous culture has alienated us. Suddenly, human consciousness, which previously alienated our species from 'unconscious nature' and from our animal selves, is nature at work in us. Snyder puts it like this: 'Consciousness, mind, imagination *and* language are fundamentally wild. "Wild" as in wild ecosystems – richly interconnected, interdependent, and incredibly complex. Diverse, ancient, and full of information' (Snyder 1995: 168). Snyder speaks of 'language as wild system, mind as wild habitat, world as a "making" (poem), poem as a creature of the wild mind' (Snyder 1995: 172). Snyder's poem 'Ripples on the Surface' celebrates 'Nature not a book, but a *performance*, a / high old culture' and ends with an image of 'The little house in the wild, / the wild in the house'. The poem thus ends by making the final integration that gives Snyder's selected poems its title: *No Nature* (1992).

This is the reverse side of the proposition that nature is culture. In Britain this is literally true, as the writings of Oliver Rackham and Richard Mabey are still revealing to us. The magnificent beech plantations of the Chiltons were planted for the Windsor chair industry, Mabey tells us, but they are being 'put into intensive care' at present as 'totems here, mythologised to an extent that their real history does not warrant'. The phrase 'Chilton beechwoods' carries a certain cultural respect that might be called Arcadian. But, in fact, all references to nature, and not just Arcadian ones, are culturally constructed. This is not to say, as some deconstructionist Romantic scholars have done, that there is 'no nature' in the sense of 'nothing we can agree upon by our use of the word' (Liu 1989: 38). On the contrary, Snyder's contention is that everything is ultimately a product of natural processes. Post-pastoral writers such as Peter Redgrove and David Abram suggest that it is important that we reconnect with it through our direct sensuous apprehension of it that is prior to language. But as soon as we use language to describe it we are inevitably using a semiology that is socially constructed and has certain inescapable cultural connotations. 'It's raining cats and dogs!' might be depressing in August in Wales, but welcomed in East Anglia, and a confirmation of madness in the English if it were said in Saudi Arabia. Individuals will want to make their personal constructions of 'It's raining cats and dogs!', but these will have to be made against their culture's generally agreed meaning of the phrase. This is the basis upon which the pastoral was founded. Arcadia was recognisably a literary construct – nature as culture.

So the fourth quality of post-pastoral literature is to convey an awareness of both nature as culture and of culture as nature. To see culture as nature is to shift from Thoreau's 'I wish to say a word for Nature' (culture representing the voiceless nature), to Aldo Leopold's 'Thinking like a mountain' (culture empathising nature), to Snyder's *No Nature* (all culture is nature). To Gary Snyder, the making of a satellite is of the same order as the making of a bird's nest, although it remains crucial to distinguish those creations of human culture which bring us closer to nature, such as Henry Moore's sculpture, or *The Winter's Tale*, and those human creations which might separate us from nature forever, such as the nuclear warheads in the submarines in Sorley MacLean's 'Screapadal'. In *Remains of Elmet* (1979) Ted Hughes suggests quite simply in one poem's title, 'Dead Farms, Dead Leaves', that the abandoned farms of the Calder Valley are the dead leaves of a stage of the human enterprise there. The chimneys of abandoned mills that sprang up like flowers, also like flowers 'must fall into the only future, into earth'. In these images the ebbs and flows of culture are natural flux in the post-pastoral sense.

The Scottish nature writer Jim Crumley sums up the way in which a culture (and its conscience) can become defined by nature in his book *Among Mountains* (1993):

We berate the fellers of tropical rainforests, the despoilers of polar wilderness, the slayers of whales, the puncturers of the ozone layer. But who should heed us, we who preside over the near extinction of our native pine forest; we who poison our own eagles; we who strangle our own mountains?

Yet we, the race of people we call Scots, *are* the mountains. Their landscape is what others judge us by, and whether we think of ourselves as Highlander or Lowlander or Islander or something else, we all look to them as the unyielding granite in the backbone of our nation. We are shaped by them. They have given us our stoicism, our reputation for hospitable shelter, our temperament of storms.

For Matthew Arnold, language and culture was what kept us above the anarchy of nature's wild armies on our 'darkling plain'. But if culture is nature and language is wildness at work, we can now find our place among what we know to be a creative–destructive world out there, in here, on the 'darkling plain'. Indeed, it is our consciousness which gives us our conscience, our ability to take responsibility for our behaviour towards the other species of the plain and towards the plain itself. One of the turning points towards the realisation of this fifth post-pastoral quality in literature, that with consciousness comes conscience, is (in what is now emerging as a test-case species) D. H. Lawrence's poem 'Snake' (1923). In this poem, consciousness ('the voice of my education') is transformed into conscience ('I thought how paltry, how vulgar, what a mean act!') as awe is transformed into humility and then into guilt at the speaker's barbarous behaviour in throwing a log at the visiting snake. The poem ends:

And so, I missed my chance with one of the lords
Of life.
And I have something to expiate;
A pettiness.

The most recent extension of the logical outcomes from Lawrence's turning point here is Rick Bass's book-length conscience-stirring essay *Fiber* (1998). Its postmodern form deceives the reader as a tactic for stimulating engagement with the conservation of his home valley, the Yaak in north-western Montana. The narrator has been a geologist 'who takes', an artist 'who gives', an activist who is tired of fighting, and now a strangely subversive 'log fairy' who at night places a different species of log in already loaded loggers' trucks. At first the narrator seems a conventional logger, but increasingly he seems as hidden and furtive as the Unabomber (if less violent), whose seventeen-year campaign against bio-technology from a remote cabin in Montana left three people dead from his letter-bombs. But suddenly the author seems to take over from the narrator: 'There is, of course, no story: no broken law back in Louisiana, no warrant, no fairy logs. I am no fugitive, other than from myself. Here, the story falls away. It – storytelling – has gotten so damn weak and safe.' A tirade about the way national conservation groups have ignored the Yaak Valley concludes, 'If you think I'm going to say *please* after what they've already done to this landscape, you can think again.' Hearing his own voice as that of 'a snarling wolverine, snapping illogically at everything in my pain', he comes to a crucial turning point. Rick Bass broke down whilst reading this story when he came to these words at the second conference of the Association for the Study of Literature and Environment (ASLE) in Missoula, Montana, a year before the book was published:

> I am going to ask for help, after all. I have to ask for help. This valley gives and gives and gives. It has been giving more timber to the country, for the last fifty years, than any other valley in the Lower 48, and still not one acre of it is protected as wilderness.

What has begun as a mysterious and gripping fiction ends with a plea for the reader to write to a dozen addresses on behalf of the Yaak. President Clinton's address tops the list. Within fifty pages Bass has written a masterpiece of the post-pastoral.

Ultimately, consciousness, which has for centuries appeared to set us apart from nature, could be seen from a biocentric point of view to be the species' opportunity to take responsibility for its ecological relationships and its ultimate survival. The role for the georgic (such as Bass's logger's story) now becomes, not the elaboration of good work practices, but a plea for environmentally sensitive local and global management.

The sixth element of post-pastoral writing is the ecofeminists' realisation that the exploitation of the planet is of the same mind-set as the exploitation of women and minorities. The gift of conscience, given us by the form of consciousness of our species, must address both environmental and social exploitation at the same time if there is to be social justice *and* a place for it to be practised. The divisiveness of our social life, in other words, derives from the same source and hubris as our divisiveness from our home. The desire to heal our relationship with the earth we inhabit must accompany the healing of our relationship with ourselves as a species. To the ecofeminists there would be no point in liberating women from exploitation if there were no healthy unpolluted planet for us to inhabit together. 'Together' is the key word, for it includes not only males (and as a post-feminist discourse some of the major contributors to ecofeminism are male critics such as Patrick Murphy), but also our fellow species. Some ecocritics are now turning towards particular aspects of our relationships with other parts of nature in literature, such as animals or mountains, in order to deconstruct and discuss our assumptions about our relationships with them that are located in our representations of them in our literature.

The development of ecofeminist theory includes writers from a wide range of disciplines, from anthropology, the history of science, economics, environmentalism, witchcraft practices and literary criticism, and has grown over the last twenty years, largely in the USA where two substantial ecofeminist essay collections have been published (Plant 1989; Diamond and Orenstein 1990). But the different ideas from which it is derived have been developed, often independently, over the last twenty years, so that one can point to some works which were not intended to be ecofeminist texts, but which might now be described as such. Caryl Churchill and Debjani Chatterjee might be surprised to find certain of their texts described as ecofeminist, but Churchill's radio play 'Not Not Not Not Not Enough Oxygen' (*Shorts* 1990) and Chatterjee's poem 'Ganapati' (*I Was That Woman* 1989) share this sixth aspect of post-pastoral literature that is also the basis of ecofeminism: that concern for the exploitation of people (in terms of gender, class and race) must accompany concern for the environment (in terms of species, elements and atmosphere) and vice versa.

An intentionally ecofeminist text such as Starhawk's poem which concludes her chapter in the ecofeminist reader *Reweaving the World* (Diamond and Orenstein 1990) can be crudely didactic. But Lorraine Anderson's marvellous anthology *Sisters of the Earth* (1991) contains many examples from the best American women writers about nature who might be called ecofeminist: Terry Tempest Williams, Linda Hogan, Paula Gunn Allen, Annie Dillard, Alice Walker, Pattiann Rogers and Ann Zwinger are all well-known names in American nature writing. The poetry of Adrienne Rich in the 1986 collection *Your Native Land, Your Life* exemplifies what Lin Nelson has called, 'the damaged woman in the damaged environment'. Rich writes, 'The problem is / to connect, without hysteria, the pain / of any one's body with the pain of the body's world'. For many post-pastoral ecofeminist writers, Arcadia might be located within the body, were 'the body's world' less damaged, environmentally and socially. To imagine an Arcadian utopia when, as Rich puts it in 'Poetry: III',

                    the children were all asleep
            and healthy   the ledgers balanced   the water running
            clear in the pipes

                              and all the prisoners free,
    is to ask

            would we give ourselves
            more calmly over   feel less criminal joy
            when the thing comes   as it does come

In Britain, Caryl Churchill's radio play 'Not Not Not Not
Not Enough Oxygen', which was first broadcast in 1971, is a rare
example of an environmental play. Its post-pastoral quality lies in
its concern for the effect upon relationships in the tower blocks of
'the Londons' of 2010, when the smog outside makes an oxygen
spray a luxury item. Churchill shows speech deteriorating along
with emotional family life in a city so polluted that people are
prisoners in their allocated single room. Claude has apparently
come to see his father for the last time before he commits suicide,
having failed to have any success as a subversive. Despite its
brevity, this is a moving and poetic play.

The Indian poet Debjani Chatterjee, who lives in England, has
brought into English literature the Hindu folklore of the elephant-
headed god of wisdom (and of literature), Ganapati. The poem
of that name addresses the god's mother, the goddess of the
Himalayas who married the god Shiva:

> Parvati, because you loved us, you bade us love the world a little.
> Radiant goddess of the mountains, you married the outcast god
> > who haunted cemeteries.
> We saw that we should embrace the children of two races:
> they are the strong links of connection and bear your blessing,
> they are rainbows spanning gulfs of silence, swamps of
> > intolerance.
> You wanted to stretch our notions of humanity.

The races of the upper (mountain) world and the lower (cemetery) worlds should be embraced in a gesture that would span 'swamps of intolerance'. Embracing the forces of life and death in nature should lead to a moral expansion so that the very notion of humanity is extended. By the end of the poem this comes to imply the inclusion of all organic nature in a concept of humanity which has now expanded to mean both 'that of which we are a part' and 'that to which we extend humane concern'.

> Ganapati, because he loved us bade us love the world a little.
> Radiant god, he married the bashful banana tree with its veil of
> > fertile leaves.
> You celebrated this union and gave your blessing.
> All the world loves a bride – we joined in and draped
> our friend's elegant wife in a red bordered sari, we blew conch shells.
> We stretched our notions of humanity.

To European anthropocentric traditions a marriage between the elephant and the banana tree might present a conceptual challenge, but the series of bonds being developed in this poem, between the animal and the human, between life and death, between the organic and the divine is based upon the Hindu belief that, as the poet herself has explained, 'with each combination that we recognise we're enriched more than the simple sum of the two halves, so our humanity is stretched'. The 'swamps of intolerance' challenged in this poem are not just those of the caste system in the opening contrast of mountain and cemetery, or the racism under implicit attack from an Indian poet published in England, but, in the address to a female god by a female poet, an intolerance for the most stretching holistic concepts upon which ecofeminism is founded.

It may have taken a contribution to British post-pastoral nature poetry from an Asian author to show Europeans that the modish call of the 1970s for radicalism to move 'from red to green' was misplaced. Socialist and feminist concerns need not displace each other, but can both be explored in literature in relation to environmentalism. Exploitation, problematic as it is in considering our economic relationship with our planetary environment, has led to the alienation which the pastoral sought to heal through the borderland imaginative space of Arcadia. It was no coincidence that the issue of gender relationships and sexual exploitation was high on the agenda in the Arcadias of Drayton, Fletcher and Shakespeare. The retreat to Arcadia for those playwrights sharpened their focus on our alienation from ourselves. Today the focus now includes an anxiety about our alienation from nature as well. In 1980 Raymond Williams wrote, 'If we alienate the living process of which we are a part, we end, though unequally, by alienating ourselves' (Williams 1980: 84). It is this urgent problem with which the sixth aspect of post-pastoral literature seeks to engage.

By way of summary of the six qualities of post-pastoral it might be helpful to illustrate their presence in a single book. This could be chosen from any one of a range of post-pastoral authors whose work has been touched upon so far: Blake, Wordsworth, Muir, Thoreau, Lawrence, Le Guin, MacLean, Heaney, Clarke and Rich. But perhaps the major achievement of contemporary post-pastoral to date is Ted Hughes's mythic sequence of poems *Cave Birds* (1978). It is an interesting case because it begins and ends with a critique of the pastoral. The cockerel protagonist is put on trial for the neglect of his inner self and his alienation from the forces of nature in himself and outside himself. 'The hero's cockerel innocence, it turns out, becomes his guilt,' Hughes said in the original 1975 radio broadcast. 'His own self, finally, the innate nature of his flesh and blood, brings him to court.' The choice of a cockerel, the archetypal image of arrogance, to represent a human hero, hints at the lack of humility derived from awe at natural processes (first post-pastoral element) that is immediately displayed in the complacently pastoral way the hero responds to death in the first poem. His facing and accepting his own death in the poem 'The Knight' marks his recognition of a creative–destructive universe of which he is a part (second post-pastoral element). The endorsement of this in showing him the role of the worm in 'A Green Mother' has already been referred to in the last chapter. The way inner nature is 'exquisitely fitted' to outer nature, and the fact that processes of outer nature are taking place in human inner nature (third post-pastoral element), is subtly suggested by the poem 'Bride and Groom Lie Hidden for Three Days'.

In this poem Hughes boldly uses images of fitting pieces of machinery together with a sense of wonder that becomes erotic when one realises that these pieces are parts of the body that 'she' gives to 'him' and 'he' gives to 'her'. This mechanical imagery prevents sentimentality or idealisation whilst biologically endorsing the symbolism of a marriage of the inner to the outer, of the self to nature. At the sexual climax of this poem 'they bring each other to perfection'. Their ecstatic completeness is compared to that of 'two gods of mud', an image that implies the vision of a god, but not one that is transcendentally above the mud of the marvellous material world. In *Cave Birds* Hughes is making a myth about the essence of material nature with an awareness that nature is mediated by culture. He is also using this myth to reconnect us to the nature in ourselves, knowing that culture is nature, in that his myth, his imaginative act, is an act of our natural capacity to heal our alienation from nature and from ourselves (fourth post-pastoral element).

In the final poem, 'The Risen', the cockerel is reborn as a falcon, an image of self-possession and predatory power. The regaining of full consciousness in this poem is also to find a renewal of conscience (fifth post-pastoral element): 'His each wingbeat – a convict's release. / What he brings will be plenty.' The final lines of the whole sequence are the two-line coda: 'At the end of the ritual / up comes a goblin', as though self-knowledge is never complete, nor free, as we shall see, from the goblin tempting a reversion to complacency. The last lines of 'The Risen' are, 'But when will he land / on a man's wrist.' This is curious in several senses: it is a statement not a question; 'a man' has not been present in the sequence; and what is its meaning in terms of the allegory? That it is a statement suggests an ironic inevitability to the human tendency to want to control nature again. The image is from the human activity of falconry, suggesting that, although the cockerel protagonist may have achieved the wholeness of this falcon, readers may now step outside the allegory and may typically want to ask this question. So these lines are the goblin raising the old hubris of human desire to control and exploit the wild energy of nature. At an allegorical level these lines represent that hubris as a fascist 'will to power', the complacent, unquestioning macho desire to exploit both social groups and natural 'resources' (sixth post-pastoral element). The male protagonist of this 'ritual' poem sequence had found that, as Hughes put it, 'the innate nature of his flesh and blood brings him to court'. This goblin suggests that he may not have learned all there is to learn about the consequences of his hubris. The cockerel of the narrative may have done, but the human he represents may not be able to resist a reversion to the complacency of the pastoral attitude expressed in the first poem of the sequence.

Of course, one of the extensions of the post-pastoral is specifically 'green' literature that engages directly with environmental issues. There have been some impressive green poems published in recent years that indicate the variety of forms this poetry can take. Tony Harrison's Gulf War poem that had its starting point in the famous newspaper photograph of an oiled cormorant, 'Initial Illumination', is a topical green poem. Philip Gross's Brechtian fable, 'What This Hand Did' is an apocalyptic poem based upon 'This Is the House that Jack Built'. In a futuristic apocalyptic poem, 'On the Beach at Cambridge', Adrian Mitchell reports from the beach, after a rise in sea level, that the ash washing ashore is not just from the burned books in Cambridge, but all the children of Cambridge, and of America, and of Russia. A rare example of a successful didactic green poem would be David Craig's 'Against Looting', which links a concern for natural 'resources' with a concern for human exploitation. The danger that green literature becomes didactic in a simplistic way is really a danger that it loses its power as art and becomes reductive propaganda or vague 'right-on' rhetoric. There is a point at which green literature can become a contemporary form of Leo Marx's 'sentimental pastoral'.

The idealisation of the whale in Heathcote Williams's long poem *Whale Nation* (1988) is an example of green poetry that goes so far as to suggest that whales are a morally higher form of life than humans and that they are therefore more worthy of 'saving' than our own species. The lavishly illustrated production of this long poem might suggest a coffee-table pastoralism, but the documentation contained in the well-researched pictures and the supporting material is a good example of the scientifically informed literature that is needed now if the sentimental pastoral is to accede to the post-pastoral. *Whale Nation* ultimately fails by taking an implicitly anti-human stance. *Falling for a Dolphin* (1988), which quickly followed the success of *Whale Nation*, is both better poetry and a better poem, although it is based upon the pastoral journey of 'dolphin therapy': a holiday swim with a dolphin in Ireland's Dingle Bay. This poem, however, eludes the charge of escapism by including the context of the author's retreat, including the cynical comments of the local fishermen about 'the fuckin' dolphin'. In meeting the dolphin Williams confronts his fear and the sea's cold to return with an enlarged view of both internal and external nature. This qualifies the poem for Leo Marx's category of 'complex pastoral'.

At this point a number of questions arise. Has the literal pastoral of travel writing, such as *Falling for a Dolphin*, now replaced the literary pastoral of Arcadia? Is Arcadia a device that can produce 'complex pastoral' today, or has the post-pastoral eclipsed classical pastoral as a viable form? If postmodernism has blurred literary categories, is there any viability in the notion of a borderland literature of retreat into nature? Is not all literature borderland now? Given the new foregrounding of 'environment', is a retreat into nature through which to explore social and moral issues even possible if it is not to be escapist pastoral in the pejorative sense? Certainly, in this pejorative use of the term, there is still an apparent need for comfortable, complacent pastoral writing in regional poetry anthologies of the British countryside, in the popularity of Richard Adams's novel *Watership Down*, in the Royal Shakespeare Company's dramatisation of Flora Thompson's *Lark Rise to Candleford* trilogy, or in the saccharined nature poetry of Californian US Poet Laureate Robert Haas (*Praise* 1979), and in Maya Angelou's poem for the inauguration of President Clinton, 'On the Pulse of Morning'.

Andrew Lawson has argued that 'in a modern society of sundered selves', the very tension of self and community, variety and unity is what 'modern pastoral is incapable, yet oddly prescient of' (Lawson 1991: 41). Answering Barrell and Bull's suggestion that the pastoral impulse faded away after the Georgians, Lawson argued that 'it simply went "underground"' to resurface as 'philosophical pastoral' in Cambridge in the 1970s, especially in the poetry of Andrew Crozier. Taking his lead from Paul de Man, Lawson offers the 'supreme modernist disenchantment' and 'a sensual scepticism pending further illumination' in the work of Crozier, Peter Riley and J. H. Prynne as a 'philosophical pastoral' of eternal deferment. This, Lawson seems to admit, will not answer to an ecological crisis in the manner of literature discussed in Lawrence Buell's recent essay 'Toxic Discourse' (1998), for example. Furthermore, it becomes a form of nostalgia for modernist scepticism that is perilously close to 'sentimental pastoral'.

But one is left asking whether modern texts that might have performed a classic pastoral function in the past, Charles Frazier's impressive first novel *Cold Mountain* (1996), A. R. Ammons's *Selected Poems* (1986), or Rebecca Solnit's travel book about the

Nevada Test Site and Yosemite National Park, *Savage Dreams* (1994), are, in fact, post-pastoral in their rejection of Arcadia in favour of a more knowing, even, in the latter case, adversarial, sense of 'environment' rather than 'nature', or 'the countryside', or 'landscape'. It is hard to avoid the conclusion that, whilst 'sentimental pastoral' is not dead, 'complex pastoral' must now take the form of post-pastoral literature.

When Leo Marx, like Buell together with Barrell and Bull, argued that the classic form of pastoral is now dead, he pointed out that 'the demise of the old pastoral in effect had liberated the mentality it had been designed to express'. 'The essence of the mode', wrote Marx, 'does not reside in any particular form or convention or body of conventions' (Marx 1986: 46). Recognising that herdsmen, with whom the origin of the form is associated, 'moved back and forth across the borderland between civilisation and nature', Marx suggested that the essence of pastoralism is 'a dialectical mode of perception' (Marx 1986: 44). The continuing need for a literature that explores our impulse towards retreat and return is likely to become stronger for the very reasons that Barrell and Bull declared the pastoral dead in English poetry after Hardy. If our lives now lack a separation between urban and rural existence, we need a post-pastoral literature that will help us understand that dialectical experience and how we can take responsibility for it. Against necessary notions of roots, neighbourhood and community there is another necessary impulse towards retreat, renewal and return. This is the circle of postmodern mobility. The paradox with which the post-pastoral engages is the fact that retreat informs our sense of community, and at a time when we are conscious of the need to improve our relationship with our neighbours on this planet, no literature could be more important to our imaging our very survival.

BIBLIOGRAPHY

Abram, David (1996) *The Spell of the Sensuous*, New York: Vintage.

Alpers, Paul (1982) 'What Is Pastoral?', *Critical Enquiry*, 8: 437–60.

—— (1996) *What Is Pastoral?*, Chicago: University of Chicago Press.

Barrell, John and Bull, John (eds) (1974) *The Penguin Book of English Pastoral Verse*, London: Allen Lane.

Bate, Jonathan (1991) *Romantic Ecology: Wordsworth and the Environmental Tradition*, London: Routledge.

Blunden, Edmund (1929) *Nature in English Literature*, London: Hogarth Press.

Buell, Lawrence (1989) 'American Pastoral Ideology Appraised', *American Literary History*, 1, 1: 1–29.

—— (1995) *The Environmental Imagination: Thoreau, Nature Writing, and the Formation of American Culture*, Cambridge, MA: Harvard University Press.

—— (1998) 'Toxic Discourse', *Critical Enquiry*, 24: 639–65.

Cavaliero, Glen (1977) *The Rural Tradition in the English Novel 1900–1939*, London: Macmillan.

Chaudhuri, Sukanta (1989) *Renaissance Pastoral and its English Developments*, Oxford: Clarendon Press.

Cooper, Helen (1977) *Pastoral: Medieval into Renaissance*, Ipswich: D. S. Brewer.

Craig, David (1987) *Native Stones*, London: Secker & Warburg.

—— (1990) *On The Crofters' Trail*, London: Jonathan Cape.

Diamond, Irene and Orenstein, Gloria Feman (eds) (1990) *Reweaving the World: The Emergence of Ecofeminism*, San Francisco: Sierra Club Books.

Empson, William (1935) *Some Versions of Pastoral*, London: Chatto & Windus.

Ford, Boris (ed.) (1955) *The Pelican Guide to English Literature: The Age of Shakespeare*, Harmondsworth: Penguin.

Foster, John (1997) *Valuing Nature? Ethics, Economics and the Environment*, London: Routledge.

Garber, Frederick (1988) 'Pastoral Spaces', *Texas Studies in Literature and Language*, 30: 431–60.

Gifford, Terry (ed.) (1992) *John Muir: The Eight Wilderness-Discovery Books*, London: Diadem.

—— (1995) *Green Voices: Understanding Contemporary Nature Poetry*, Manchester: Manchester University Press.

—— (1996) 'Dialogues', *Real Differences*, Carlisle: Tullie House Museum and Art Gallery.

—— (1997) *The Climbers' Club Centenary Journal*, Leicester: Cordee.

Heaney, Seamus (1980) *Preoccupations*, London: Faber & Faber.

Henke, Robert (1997) *Pastoral Transformations: Italian Tragicomedy and Shakespeare's Late Plays*, London: Associated University Presses.

Herzfeld, Michael (1985) *The Poetics of Manhood: Contest and Identity in a Cretan Mountain Village*, Princeton, NJ: Princeton University Press.

Hooker, Jeremy (1996) *Writers in a Landscape*, Cardiff: University of Wales Press.

Hunter, G. K. (1962) *John Lily*, London: Routledge.

Keith, W. J. (1975) *The Rural Tradition: A Study of Non-Fiction Prose Writers of the English Countryside*, Brighton: Harvester.

Landry, Donna (1990) *The Muses of Resistance: Laboring-Class Women's Poetry in Britain, 1739–1796*, Cambridge: Cambridge University Press.

Lawson, Andrew (1991) 'On Modern Pastoral', *Fragmente*, 3: 35–41.

Liu, Alan (1989) *Wordsworth: The Sense of History*, Stanford, CA: Stanford University Press.

Lloyd, A. L. (1967) *Folk Song in England*, London: Lawrence & Wishart.

Loughrey, Bryan (ed.) (1984) *The Pastoral Mode*, London: Macmillan.

Lucas, John (1990) *England and Englishness*, London: Hogarth Press.

Marinelli, Peter V. (1971) *Pastoral*, London: Methuen.

Marx, Leo (1964) *The Machine in the Garden: Technology and the Pastoral Ideal in America*, New York: Oxford University Press.

—— (1986) 'Pastoralism in America', in Sacvan Bercovitch and Myra Jehlen (eds) *Ideology and Classic American Literature*, Cambridge: Cambridge University Press.

Merchant, Carolyn (1980) *The Death of Nature: Women, Ecology, and the Scientific Revolution*, New York: Harper & Row.

Murphy, Patrick D. (1995) *Literature, Nature, and Other*, New York: SUNY.

Nash, Roderick (1989) *The Rights of Nature*, Madison: University of Wisconsin Press.

Nemo, John (1979) *Patrick Kavanagh*, London: George Prior.

Panofsky, Erwin (1970) *Meaning in the Visual Arts*, Harmondsworth: Penguin.

Patterson, Annabel (1987) *Pastoral and Ideology: Virgil to Valery*, Berkeley: University of California Press.

Plant, Judith (ed.) (1989) *Healing the Wounds: The Promise of Ecofeminism*, Philadelphia: New Society Publishers.

Radin, Paul (1956) *The Trickster*, London: Routledge.

Roberts, Neil (1994) *The Lover, the Dreamer and the World: The Poetry of Peter Redgrove*, Sheffield: Sheffield Academic Press.

Robertson, David (1984) *West of Eden: A History of the Art and Literature of Yosemite*, Yosemite Natural History Association and Wilderness Press.

Rooda, Randall (1998) *Dramas of Solitude: Narratives of Retreat in American Nature Writing*, New York: State University of New York Press.

Rosaldo, Michelle and Lamphere, Louise (eds) (1974) *Woman, Culture, and Society*, Stanford, CA: Stanford University Press.

Ross, J. R. and Hendry, Joy (1986) *Sorley MacLean: Critical Essays*, Edinburgh: Scottish Academic Press.

Sales, Roger (1983) *English Literature in History 1780–1830: Pastoral and Politics*, London: Hutchinson.

Scheese, Don (1996) *Nature Writing: The Pastoral Impulse in America*, New York: Twayne.

Scigaj, Leonard M. (1996) 'Contemporary Ecological and Environmental Poetry: *Différance* or *Référance?*, *ISLE (Interdisciplinary Studies in Literature and Environment)* 3, 2: 1–25.

—— (1999) *Sustainable Poetry: Four American Ecopoets*, Lexington, KY: University of Kentucky.

Short, Brian (ed.) (1992) *The English Rural Community: Image and Analysis*, Cambridge: Cambridge University Press.

Smith, Stan (1986) *Edward Thomas*, London: Faber & Faber.

Snyder, Gary (1992) *The Practice of the Wild*, New York: Pantheon Books.

—— (1995) *A Place in Space*, Washington, DC: Counterpoint.

Szatek, Karoline P. (1995) 'The Discourse of Space and Perception in the English Renaissance Pastoral Dramas', unpublished PhD thesis, Indiana University of Pennsylvania.

Thomson, Derick (1977) *An Introduction to Gaelic Poetry*, London: Gollancz.

Wallis, Lawrence B. (1968) *Fletcher, Beaumont and Company*, New York: Octagon Books.

Williams, Raymond (1975) *The Country and the City*, London: Chatto & Windus.

—— (1980) *Problems in Materialism and Culture*, London: Verso.

INDEX